CONTENTS

Preface 7

Aquatic plants and their ecological importance 9

Nutrient cycle in a lake 9

Zonation of water plants 10

    The water margins 11

    Emergent plants 12

    Floating-leaved plants 12

    Submerged plants 13

Plant plankton (phytoplankton) 14

Attached organisms 18

Explanation of some botanical features used in identification 20

Keys for identification 22

Emergent plants 22

Floating-leaved plants 26

Submerged plants 28

Descriptions of water plants 31

Emergent plants 31

    Horsetail, *Equisetum* 31

    Marsh Horsetail, *Equisetum palustre* L. 31

    Water Horsetail, *Equisetum fluviatile* L. 31

    Reedmace, *Typha* 33

    Great Reedmace, *Typha latifolia* L. 33

    Lesser Reedmace, *Typha angustifolia* L. 33

    Bur-reed, *Sparganium erectum* L. 35

    Unbranched Bur-reed, *Sparganium emersum* Rehm............ 35

    Water Plantain, *Alisma plantago-aquatica* L. 37

    Arrow-head, *Sagittaria sagittifolia* L. 37

    Flowering Rush, *Butomus umbellatus* L. 40

    Reed-grass, *Phalaris arundinacea* L. 40

    Reed, *Phragmites communis* Trinius........................ 42

    Scolochloa festucacea Link 44

    Reed-grass, or Great Water Grass, *Glyceria maxima* (Hartm.)

        Holmb... 44

Flote-grass, *Glyceria fluitans* (L.) R. Br. 46
Bulrush, *Schoenoplectus lacustris* (L.) Palla 46
Common Spike-rush, *Eleocharis palustris* (L.) Roem & Schult .. 49
Sedges, *Carex* L. 49
Tufted Sedge, *Carex acuta* L. 50
Cyperus Sedge, *Carex pseudocyperus* L. 50
Beaked Sedge, *Carex rostrata* Stokes........................ 50
Great Pond-sedge, *Carex riparia* Curtis 50
Bog Arum, *Calla palustris* L. 50
Sweet Flag, *Acorus calamus* L. 52
Rushes, *Juncus*.. 52
Soft Rush, *Juncus effusus* L. 54
Conglomerate Rush, *Juncus conglomeratus* L. 54
Hard Rush, *Juncus inflexus* L. 54
Yellow Flag, *Iris pseudacorus* L. 54
Great Water Dock, *Rumex hydrolaphatum* Hudson 56
Water-pepper, *Polygonum hydropiper* L. 56
Marsh Marigold, Kingcup, *Caltha palustris* L. 56
Great Spearwort, *Ranunculus lingua* L. 56
Great Yellow-cress, *Rorippa amphibia* (L.) Bess. 59
Water-cress, *Rorippa nasturtium-aquaticum* (L.) Hay 60
Purple Loosestrife, *Lythrum salicaria* L...................... 61
Mare's-tail, *Hippuris vulgaris* L. 61
Large Bitter-cress, *Cardamine amara* L. 63
Cowbane, *Cicuta virosa* L. 63
Water-parsnip, *Sium latifolium* L. 64
Narrow-leaved Water-parsnip, *Berula erecta* (Huds.) Coville ... 66
Fine-leaved Water Dropwort, *Oenanthe aquatica* (L.) Poiret 66
Creeping Jenny, *Lysimachia nummularia* L. 68
Tufted Loosestrife, *Naumburgia thyrsiflora* (L.) Reichenbach ... 69
Yellow Loosestrife, *Lysimachia vulgaris* L. 69
Bogbean, *Menanythes trifoliata* L........................... 69
Water Forget-me-not, *Myosotis scorpioides* L. 71
Common Skull-cap, *Scutellaria galericulata* L. 72
Marsh Woundwort, *Stachys palustris* L. 74
Gipsy-wort, *Lycopus europaeus* L. 75
Water Mint, *Mentha aquatica* L. 76
Bittersweet, Woody Nightshade, *Solanum dulcamara* L. 77
Brooklime, *Veronica beccabunga* L. 78

4

Water Speedwell, *Veronica anagallis-aquatica* L. 78
Trifid Bur-marigold, *Bidens tripartita* L. 79
Nodding Bur-marigold, *Bidens cernua* L. 79

Floating-leaved Plants 80

Floating Crystalwort, *Riciella fluitans* L. 80
Water Fern, *Salvinia natans*, Allioni 80
Fairy Moss, *Azolla filiculoides* Lam. 80
Broad-leaved Pondweed, *Potamogeton natans* L. 82
Various-leaved Pondweed, *Potamogeton gramineus* L. 83
Frog-bit, *Hydrocharis morsus-ranae* L. 84
Duckweeds, *Lemna, Wolffia* 85
Duckweed, *Lemna minor* L. 85
Great Duckweed, *Lemna polyrrhiza* L. 86
Gibbous Duckweed, *Lemna gibba* L. 86
Ivy Duckweed, *Lemna trisulca* L. 86
Least Duckweed, *Wolffia arrhiza* (L.) Hook ex Wimm 86
Amphibious Bistort, *Polygonum amphibium* L. 86
White Water-lily, *Nymphaea alba* L. 87
Yellow Water-lily, *Nuphar lutea* (L.) Smith 89
Water-Crowfoots, *Ranunculus* spp. 91
Water-Crowfoot, *Ranunculus aquatilis* L. 92
Water Chestnut, *Trapa natans* L. 92
Fringed Water-lily, *Nymphoides peltata* (Gmel). O.Kuntze 93

Submerged Plants 95

Stoneworts, *Chara* spp. and *Nitella* spp. 95
Willow Moss, *Fontinalis antipyretica* L. 97
Quillwort, *Isoetes lacustris* L. 98
Pondweeds, *Potamogeton* 99
Shining Pondweed, *Potamogeton lucens* L. 100
Perfoliate Pondweed, *Potamogeton perfoliatus* L. 101
Curly Pondweed, *Potamogeton crispus* L. 102
Grass-wrack Pondweed, *Potamogeton compressus* L. 103
Grassy Pondweed, *Potamogeton obtusifolius* Mert. et Koch 104
Fennel-leaved Pondweed, *Potamogeton pectinatus* L. 105
Holly-leaved Naiad, *Najas marina* L. 106
Water Soldier, *Stratiotes aloides* L. 107
Canadian Pondweed, *Elodea canadensis* Michaux 108

Slender Spike-rush, *Eleocharis acicularis* (L.) R. et Schult 109
Hornwort, *Ceratophyllum demersum* L. 111
Spineless Hornwort, *Ceratophyllum submersum* L. 112
Long-leaved Water-Crowfoot, *Ranunculus fluitans*, Lamarck ... 112
Stiff-leaved Water-Crowfoot, *Ranunculus circinatus* Sibth. 113
Water Starworts, *Callitriche* L. 114
Autumnal Starwort, *Callitriche hermaphroditica* L. 114
Callitriche platycarpa, Kütz 115
Callitriche stagnalis Scop. 116
Callitriche palustris L. 116
Waterwort, *Elatine hydropiper* L. 116
Whorled Water-milfoil, *Myriophyllum verticillatum* L. 117
Spiked Water-milfoil, *Myriophyllum spicatum* L. 118
Water Violet, *Hottonia palustris* L. 118
Greater Bladderwort, *Utricularia vulgaris* L. 120
Shore-weed, *Littorella uniflora* (L.) Aschers 121
Water Lobelia, *Lobelia dortmanna* L. 122

Bibliography 124

Index 125

PREFACE

It is the aim of this little book to convey, by means of description and illustrations, a knowledge of the more common aquatic plants that are found both in and by the water.

Most of the plants illustrated are either fairly common in the water and on the banks of lakes or rivers, or are worth noticing for their value in fishing waters.

The plants described in this book are, for convenience, divided into three groups:

> plants which emerge from the water
> plants with leaves floating on the water
> plants living submerged.

This rough-and-ready division does not take into account the many life-forms of water plants but it has been chosen purposely to fulfil the aim of the book, to serve as a simple guide for naturalists, fishermen, and others who have no special botanical knowledge.

In order to facilitate identification of the individual plants the usual systematic features have been dispensed with. Leaf shape and the overall appearance of the plants have been used, as these are often the only characters available. The popular names are those which are in common use.

Within the individual groups—emergent, floating-leaved, sub-merged—the plants have been listed in systematic order.

The bibliography contains a list of works useful for a more detailed study of water plants.

In the British edition the scientific names are based on the *Flora of the British Isles* by Clapham, Tutin and Warburg, 2nd edition.

ACKNOWLEDGEMENTS

My thanks are due to Dr. H.H. Wundsch, Dr. W. Schäperclaus and Dr. H. Beger for their kind advice and suggestions. I also wish to express my gratitude to the publishers for the trouble they have taken in preparing this book.

AQUATIC PLANTS
AND THEIR ECOLOGICAL IMPORTANCE

Plants are the only living organisms capable of building up organic matter from inorganic material. Animals do not possess this faculty, but organic matter is essential for their life. Therefore they depend on plants, either directly as herbivores or indirectly as predators. This fact is fundamental to all life, both on land and in the water.

Nutrient Cycle in a Lake

The diagram illustrates the interdependence of the various communities.

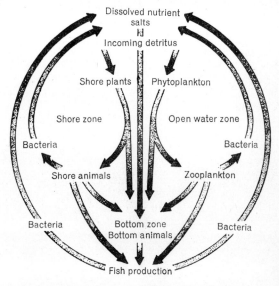

Diagram of nutrient cycle in a lake. After A. Thienemann.

Water entering a lake carries dissolved salts. Water, salts and sunlight form the basis of plant life. Only the presence of plants makes animal life possible. As organisms die, bacteria break down their bodies into simple inorganic compounds which return into circulation as nutrients.

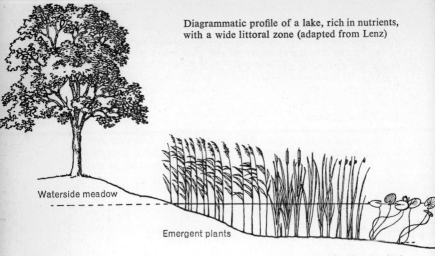

Diagrammatic profile of a lake, rich in nutrients, with a wide littoral zone (adapted from Lenz)

Waterside meadow

Emergent plants

Floating-leaved plants

After this brief explanation of the part played by plants in the interplay of life processes, we turn to a study of their requirements, both for life on land and in the water.

Zonation of Water Plants

Conditions for plant growth vary according to the type of water they inhabit. A study of aquatic plants in a lake rich in nutrients and with a wide littoral zone will show various habitats; from these considerations conclusions may be drawn about the development of plant life under different conditions. In a body of water the conditions at the bottom depend on the geological substratum, its topography, the nutrient content of the water and that of its catchment area as well as its plant and animal life. A typical zonation is characteristic of a lake rich in nutrients and with a wide littoral zone. This zonation is determined by the nature of the bottom, the depth and transparency of the water.

Passing from the area immediately surrounding the water with its typical trees, shrubs and herbs we reach the emergent plants; in most cases there follow floating plants which provide a transition to those that are totally submerged.

10

With increasing depth, illumination becomes insufficient to support plant life so that the deep lightless zone is devoid of plants.

But in the illuminated layers of the open water some plants are found, the floating or actively moving algae which are called phytoplankton. This plays an integral part in the economy of the water.

The Water Margins

The water margins with their wet soil have their own type of vegetation. Only those plants will thrive which need a great deal of

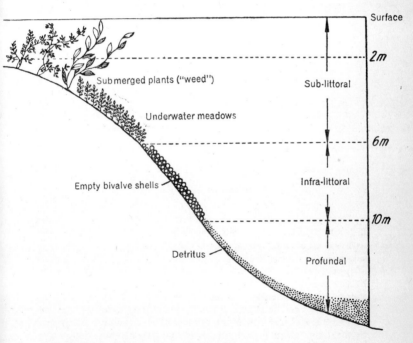

moisture and a continuous supply of water. They are specially adapted to the often fluctuating water conditions.

The willow, for instance, sends shallow roots into the ground since the deeper layers of soil are poor in oxygen, making it difficult, or even

11

impossible, for the roots to breathe. Willow trees have particularly good powers of regeneration; injuries occurring frequently at high water or through a cover of ice will heal easily. Willow cuttings are known to strike roots quickly. In addition to willows the Alder is typical of this zone around the shore; Elder, Guelder Rose and Buckthorn also occur. Among the herbs there are sedges, rushes, Woody Nightshade, Kingcup, Lesser Spearwort, Cowbane, Great Water Dock and Water Forget-me-not.

Emergent Plants

At the water's edge is the zone of emergent plants. It consists of plants whose roots and lower parts stand in water, while their leaves and flowers rise above the surface. The roots absorb nutrients from the soil, they use the carbon dioxide from the air and give off oxygen into the atmosphere, living in the manner of terrestrial plants. The emergent plants make no contribution to the nutrient cycle of the lake; nor do the dying parts represent a gain for the water. The emergent plants are rich in cellulose. They do not undergo complete decomposition from the end of one period of growth to the end of the next one; as a result the dying parts accumulate on top of those from the preceding season and the process of decay does not reach completion. An unproductive, cellulose-rich detritus is formed. The floor of the lake is constantly being raised and this is favoured by the closely interwoven root system. Here we find the beginning of the silting-up processes.

The emergent plants have some limited value; in loosely-standing groups they offer good spawning places and provide shelter for young fish. Large numbers of organisms attach themselves to their underwater parts, serving as food for the young fish and the animals on which the fish feed. Occasionally the emergent plants are a useful protection for a dam and enable the angler to do his fishing in peace.

According to conditions, the zone of emergent plants may be up to 2 metres wide.

Floating-leaved Plants

In general the floating leaves of these plants are of a leathery consistency, have an entire margin and the surface appears covered with wax so that drops of water immediately roll off.

Floating-leaved plants display some special features which make them suited to their way of life. The rooted plants such as White Water-lily, Yellow Water-lily, Amphibious Bistort and others absorb nutrient

12

salts from the soil. In plants floating freely on the water surface such as Frogbit and Duckweed the aquatic roots take up nutrients directly from the water. Carbon dioxide is absorbed through the stomata situated on the upper side of the leaf and oxygen is given off into the air.

Floating-leaved plants develop only in the quiet parts of bodies of water. The depth of the lake bottom determines the range of those rooting in the mud.

On the whole they must be considered unproductive for fishing. True, numerous animals on which fish feed are found in their underwater parts; but the leaves frequently form a continuous cover, shading the surface to such an extent that the water does not warm up and the development of animals on which fish feed is prevented. The hard consistency of the floating leaves and the frequently considerable rhizome may contribute to silting up.

Submerged Plants

The submerged plants, called "weed" by fishermen, are the most valuable in waters used for fishing. They are completely submerged and only their flowers may rise above the surface. The roots—if any—mostly serve for anchorage only, while the absorption of the nutrients dissolved in the water and that of carbon dioxide takes place over the entire, very thin surface layer. The oxygen released in photosynthesis is given off into the water, thus benefiting the water itself, the respiration of the animals, as well as promoting the decomposition of organic matter by means of bacteria requiring oxygen.

The leaves are often finely dissected into awl-shaped lobes or are ribbon-shaped, thus providing a larger surface for better assimilation of salts and gases. For the same reason the leaf surface is very thin. There is no need either for a conducting system or for stomata. Strengthening elements, that is cells in which the walls have been specially stiffened, are not needed since it is the water and not the stem which supports the leaves. But tensile strength, to withstand water currents, is safeguarded by means of special tissues situated in the centre of the plant body. Instead of or in addition to the usual process of seed production a number of other methods serve for the maintenance and reproduction of the plants.

Asexual (vegetative) reproduction is of crucial importance for submerged plants. New stands are often produced from fragments of plants (Canadian Pondweed, Hornwort). Another form of vegetative reproduction is represented by winter-buds (hibernacula). A few plants such as Water-milfoil, some Pondweeds, Hornwort, Water Soldier produce bud-like structures, containing reserve material, at the end of their

13

vegetative period; these detach themselves from the plant and sink to the bottom where they overwinter. They develop into new plants in the spring.

In waters rich in lime a sand-like cover may often be seen on the submerged plants. It consists of lime which has been deposited on the plants during photosynthesis. It is dissolved in water as calcium bicarbonate. During vigorous photosynthesis when the plant has used up the free carbon dioxide dissolved in water, the carbon reserve of the calcium bicarbonate is being utilized. It decomposes according to the formula:

$$Ca(HCO_3)_2 = CaCO_3 + H_2O + CO_2$$

As plants depend on light their penetration into deep water is determined by its transparency but some plants are able to exist at great depths and with little light. They are mainly stoneworts, as well as Canadian Pondweed, *Fontinalis* and *Najas* which cover the bottom like a carpet. Their shoots no longer reach the water surface.

The flaccid consistency of the submerged plants allows their rapid and complete decomposition. They play an essential part in the formation of a fertile detritus. They also supply oxygen to the water. The submerged plants are the most important carriers of attached organisms. (See page 8) They offer favourite spawning grounds for fish and are consumed by the animals on which fish feed; these plants, therefore, are useful for fishing waters. But it must not be forgotten that submerged plants may also have some harmful effects. If they become too abundant they hinder netting and the dying plants may produce considerable deposits of detritus which finally cause a silting of the lake bottom. In ponds and parts of the lakes sheltered from the wind large amounts of submerged plants may produce excessive quantities of oxygen, resulting in a harmful rise in pH.

Plant Plankton (Phytoplankton)

Plankton is the term used for all microscopically small animals and plants which float freely in the water. The illuminated layers of bodies of water are their habitat. The small, simplest types of plants also require light to build up their body substance by means of photosynthesis. They provide the basic organic nutrients in open water.

The large number of kinds of planktonic plants makes it impossible to give a detailed account of the various groups. But a short survey of the importance of phytoplankton and of the main forms will serve to complete the picture of plant life in water.

14

The development of these plant micro-organisms depends on the chemical composition of the water, its temperature and light conditions. As a result species composition and numbers vary greatly from one sheet of water to another. There is also a seasonal change of forms. In the summer, for instance, blue-green algae and green algae predominate, while diatoms are dominant in the winter. A knowledge of planktonic forms and their numbers allows conclusions to be drawn about the productivity of a body of water and the conditions prevailing in it. Phytoplankton is the basic food of animal plankton; after death it sinks to the bottom and provides the main part of the fertile detritus—the life element of the bottom animals.

The most varied algal groups are components of the fresh-water phytoplankton. Only a few of the main groups will be mentioned which are represented in all kinds of water.

Bacteria: The planktonic bacteria usually play a subordinate role in planktonic investigations; they are mostly so small that special methods are needed for their identification. But their important role in the water must be stressed, that is the essential part they play in breaking down the dying organisms into their basic constituents.

Blue-green Algae *(Cyanophyceae):* The blue-green algae are the simplest representatives of the algae. They have no true nucleus and reproduce by simple fission. The green pigment, chlorophyll, is often masked by bluish-green, brownish-green or reddish pigments.

There is a great variety of cellular shapes. There are unicellular types in which the cells are spherical-longate, egg-shaped, curved like an S or spiral-shaped. A gelatinous sheath often binds them together into colonies. In others the cells are joined into threads; in some all the cells are roughly similar and others show a marked differentiation into a foot and a tip.

Most blue-green algae are immobile. Certain filamentous forms carry out undulating movements. Various blue-green algae *(Aphanizomenon, Microcystis)* appear in large masses during the warm season and form a special floating layer. This is called a 'water bloom' and is often connected with a typical odour. A water bloom of *Oscillatoria* may result in the fish developing an unpleasant taste.

Flagellates: The flagellates are small, unicellular planktonic organisms which possess a true nucleus. They move actively by means of one or two flagella, depending on the species. The lowest forms have a naked cell body protected only by a denser outer covering. In the more highly organized forms the cells are surrounded by a membrane of cellulose, pectins or other material. The flagellates are either free-living or united into colonies. Some live like animals (requiring organic food), but the

15

majority are autotrophic (using inorganic food) and, like plants, have chromatophores (carriers of pigments). The flagellates reproduce asexually by binary fission; sexual reproduction is mostly by gametes of identical shape (isogametes).

Diatoms: The diatoms are brown, unicellular and surrounded by a characteristic shell of silica. The shell consists of two parts, the upper part overlapping the lower like a deep lid on a box. The diatom cell has a nucleus and brownish-yellow chromatophores.

Asexual reproduction is by means of binary fission in which the two halves of the silica shell move apart and each cell produces a new lower half. This type of reproduction results in the daughter cells becoming increasingly smaller. This process continues until a minimum size has been reached; after that the original cell size typical of any species is attained by the formation of growth spores (auxospores). In some diatoms this is always connected with sexual reproduction.

Many planktonic diatoms have special mechanisms for keeping afloat or are joined into chains by means of a gelatinous cover. Some species show jerking movement caused by protoplasmic streaming.

Green Algae *(Chlorophyceae):* The green algae have pure green pigmented bodies (chloroplasts). Both their vegetative structure and types of reproduction display extraordinary variety. The vegetative stages are always non-motile. Among the green algae there are microscopically small unicellular forms, filamentous algae forming thick tufts as well as some resembling higher plants.

The oxygen given off in photosynthesis enables the thread-like algae to float on the water surface; they often drift on the water as large green wads. The chief representatives of these filamentous algae are *Cladophora* (fig. p. 19) and *Spirogyra* (fig. p. 19) which belongs to the group of Conjugates. A rough distinction between these two algae can be made by handling the wads; those formed by *Cladophora* are hard to the touch while those made by *Spirogyra* feel soft and slippery.

The algal groups listed above contain not only planktonic forms. Many species are found at the bottom of the water and others attach themselves to some objects in the water.

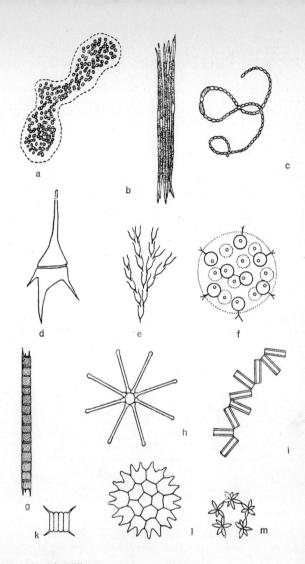

Plankton Algae (×150)
Blue-green algae *a Microcystis; b Aphanizomenon; c Anabaena*
Flagellates *d Ceratium; e Dinobryon; f Eudorina*
Diatoms *g Melosira; h Asterionella; i Diatoma*
Green algae *k Scenedesmus; l Pediastrum; m Actinastrum*

Organisms attached to *Cladophora*

Attached organisms

From the point of the biology of fisheries the attached organisms are as important as the plankton itself; many of the animals on which fish feed occur on and between the plants and eat the attached organisms.

The algae which have special means of attachment, mainly belong to the diatoms, and the green and blue-green algae. They have gelatinous stalks, gelatinous cushions or special cells at the foot which enable them to attach themselves to the substratum or else lie flat on it. In addition, quantities of amorphous organic particles (detritus) are frequently found among the attached algae; after being carried into that position they have been retained there. The attached organisms appear as a green or brownish coating which covers the submerged parts of plants.

The number of attached organisms settling on different aquatic plants varies. They are richly developed on Water-milfoil and some kinds of pondweed, while Hornwort is usually sparsely colonized. But the wealth of attached forms depends not only on the plant species; their development is also affected by local variations in the shore region.

The composition of attached organisms is subject to seasonal changes. Diatoms form the bulk in early spring (fig. p. 17) while green and blue-green algae predominate in the summer and autumn.

18

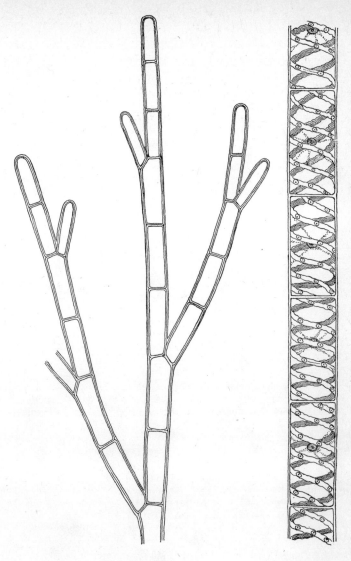

Cladophora (×125)   *Spirogyra* (×300)

19

EXPLANATION OF SOME BOTANICAL FEATURES
USED FOR IDENTIFICATION

Parts of an entire leaf

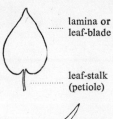

.... lamina or
leaf-blade

.... leaf-stalk
(petiole)

In grasses

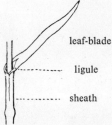

.... leaf-blade

.... ligule

.... sheath

Arrangement of leaves on stem

basal in rosette alternate opposite in whorls

Shape of leaves

entire   palmate   lobed
(margin only
saw-edged or toothed)

Compound leaves

simply pinnate

doubly pinnate

trifoliolate

Type of margin

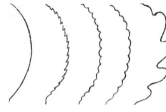

a entire
b serrate
c dentate
d crenate
e sinuate

Outline of leaf

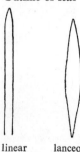

linear   lanceolate

ovate

kidney-shaped

Venation

arcuate-parallel

parallel-veined

net-veined

KEYS FOR IDENTIFICATION

Emergent Plants

Plants rising above the water surface

Plants with compound or divided leaves

The numbers on the right side of the table refer to those on the left-hand side where identification continues.

1 Leaves (mostly) in 3 parts
  Leaves in many parts   2
2 Leaves long-stalked, three-partite like clover, entire margin   3

     Bogbean *(Menyanthes trifoliata)*

  Leaves sessile, with 3 parts or divided into 5 finger-like segments, tips lance-shaped, saw-edged

     Bur-marigold *(Bidens)*

3 Leaves simply pinnate   4
  Leaves compound pinnate   7
4 Leaf segments 4–10 cm long, elongate, lance-shaped, sharply saw-edged, pointed, unequally wide at base

     Water-parsnip *(Sium latifolium)*

  Leaf segments smaller   5
5 Leaf margin with pointed saw-edge

     Narrow-leaved Water-parsnip *(Sium erectum)*

  Leaf margin not as above
6 Stem angled, hollow; leaves soft, somewhat fleshy

     Water-cress *(Rorippa nasturtium-aquatica)*

  Stem with pith, leaves harder than in last species

     Large Bitter-cress *(Cardamine amara)*

7 Leaf segments with lance-shaped-linear, sharply toothed tips
  Leaf segments of 2nd order over 1 cm broad

     Cowbane *(Cicuta virosa)*

  Leaf segments egg-shaped in outline, deeply indented, small tips with entire margin

     Fine-leaved Water Dropwort *(Oenanthe aquatica)*

22

Plants with basal leaves

1	Leaves long, narrow, not round in cross section	2
	not as above	6
2	Leaves flat	3
	Leaves linear triangular; flowers in large umbel reddish-white	

       Flowering Rush *(Butomus umbellatus)*

3	Leaves sword-shaped, gradually tapering towards the tip, distinct midrib, stiffly erect	4
	Leaves with indistinct (not protruding) midrib	5
4	Upper part of leaves with wavy margin on one side, bright green	

       Sweet Flag *(Acorus calamus)*

Leaves smooth, bluish-green

       Yellow Flag *(Iris pseudacorus)*

5 Plants over 1 m high (to about 3 m) flowers in a large spike

       Reedmace *(Typha)*

Plants less than 1 m Stem three-angled

       Sedge *(Carex)*

6	Leaves round in cross section	7
	Leaves with flat leaf blade	9
7	Plants over 1 m high, stem up to finger-thick	

       Bulrush *(Schoenoplectus lacustris)*

	Plants smaller	8
8	Inflorescence terminal	

       Common Spike-rush *(Eleocharis palustris)*

Inflorescence apparently lateral

       Rush *(Juncus)*

9 Leaves arrow-shaped, arranged in a rosette

       Arrow-head *(Sagittaria sagittifolia)*

	Leaves not as above	10
10	Leaves long-stalked, spoon-shaped, forming a rosette	

       Water Plantain *(Alisma plantago-aquatica)*

Leaves stalked, heart-shaped, not in a rosette

       Bog Arum *(Calla palustris)*

Plants with opposite or whorled leaves

1   Plants with leaves in a whorl   2
      Plants with opposite leaves   4

2   Leaves or branches 8 to 12 in a whorl   3
      Leaves mostly 3 in a whorl. Leaf elongate egg-shaped, pointed

         Yellow Loosestrife *(Lysimachia vulgaris)*

3   Leaves linear

         Mare's-tail *(Hippuris vulgaris)*

      Stems and branches consisting of overlapping internodes, surrounded by a toothed sheath at the base

         Horsetail *(Equisetum)*

4   Leaves sessile   5
      Leaves more or less stalked   8

5   Leaf margin entire   6
      not as above   7

6   Leaves on stem in whorls of 2 or 3, broadly lance-shaped, hairless

         Purple Loosestrife *(Lythrum salicaria)*

      Leaves in crossed pairs (decussate), lance-shaped, fine hairs on underside

         Tufted Loosestrife *(Naumburgia thyrsiflora)*

7   Stem round, leaves egg-lance-shaped, pointed, slightly saw-edged

         Water Speedwell *(Veronica anagallis)*

      Stem angular, leaf margin crenate-saw-edged, leaves with soft hairs

         Marsh Woundwort *(Stachys palustris)*

8   Stem round, leaves elliptical, blunt, slightly crenate-saw-edged
         Brooklime *(Veronica beccabunga)*

      Stem angular   9

9   Leaf margin entire, leaf broadly spatula-shaped
         Creeping Jenny *(Lysimachia nummularia)*

      Leaf margin crenate, saw-edged, leaf-blade partly comb-like dissected   10

10 Leaf margin coarsely toothed, leaf-blade partly comb-like dissected

    Gipsy-wort *(Lycopus europaeus)*

Leaf margin not as above   11
11 Leaves elongate lance-shaped, slightly heart-shaped at the base, leaf margin crenate

    Common Skull-cap *(Scutellaria galericulata)*

Leaves roundish, egg-shaped, heart-shaped at the base, margin crenate

    Water Mint *(Mentha aquatica)*

Plants with alternate leaves

1 Leaves grass-like, plants with nodes on stem   2
   Leaves not grass-like   6
2 Leaf sheath ending in a collar of stiff hairs. Plant up to 3 m high

    Reed *(Phragmites communis)*

Leaf sheath without a collar of hairs   3
3 Plant erect up to 2 m high; leaf gradually tapering to a point

    Scolochloa festucacea

Plant not as above   4
Plant erect, very similar to reed in its appearance. Ligule dissected

    Reed-grass *(Phalaris)*

Plants mostly creeping on ground   5
5 Plants largely erect (up to 2 m high). Leaves 1·5–2 cm broad; flower spike regularly symmetrical

    Reed-grass *(Glyceria maxima)*

Plants procumbent, leaves up to 1 cm wide; spike turned to one side

    Flote-grass *(Glyceria fluitans)*

6 Leaves triangular, flower heads spherical. Fruit resembling a rolled-up hedgehog   7
   Leaves not triangular   8
7 Leaves over 1 cm broad; inflorescence branched

    Bur-reed *(Sparganium erectum)*
   Leaves narrower; inflorescence unbranched

    Unbranched Bur-reed *(Sparganium emersum)*

25

8　Leaves broad, kidney-shaped, margin crenate
　　Leaves not as above　　　　　　　　　　　　　　　　　9
9　Leaves very large (40–100 cm long), broadly lance-shaped,
　　small flowers in dense tufts

Great Water Dock *(Rumex hydrolaphatum)*

　　Leaves not so large　　　　　　　　　　　　　　　　10
10　Stem 4-angled, leaves elongate lance-shaped, with rough hairs

Water Forget-me-not *(Myosotis scorpioides)*

　　Stem round, leaves without rough hairs　　　　　　　　11
11　Leaf margin entire　　　　　　　　　　　　　　　　12
　　Leaf margin toothed, crenate, irregularly dissected or entire,
　　elongate or lance-shaped, narrowing at the base. The lower leaves
　　often dissected in a comb-like or lyre-shaped fashion

Great Yellow Cress *(Rorippa amphibia)*

12　Leaves lance-shaped, tapering at both ends　　　　　　13
　　Leaves usually egg-shaped-lance-shaped, tapering, the upper-
　　most often spear-shaped, in three lobes. Flowers purple, berries
　　red

Bittersweet, Woody Nightshade *(Solanum dulcamara)*

13　Leaves of flowering shoots very short-stalked. Plant stiffly erect,
　　up to 1.5 m high

Great Spearwort *(Ranunculus lingua)*

　　Leaves clearly stalked, surrounding the stem with a papery
　　sheath

Water-pepper *(Polygonum hydropiper)*

Plants with floating leaves

1　Plants freely floating, not rooting at the bottom　　　　9
　　Plants rooting　　　　　　　　　　　　　　　　　　2
2　Plants having leaves with entire margin　　　　　　　　3
　　Plants with different leaves　　　　　　　　　　　　　8
3　Leaves smooth, leathery　　　　　　　　　　　　　　4
　　Leaves somewhat wavy at the margin, about 8 cm large

Fringed Water-lily *(Nymphoides peltata)*

4　Leaves round or oval, deeply lobed at the base　　　　　5
　　Leaves oblong, elliptical, not deeply lobed at base　　　6
5　Leaves round; stem round in cross section

White Water-lily *(Nymphaea alba)*

Leaves oval, stem roughly triangular in cross section
Yellow Water-lily *(Nuphar luteum)*

6 Floating leaves net-veined
Amphibious Bistort *(Polygonum amphibium)*

Floating leaves venation arcuate-parallel 7
7 Floating leaves mostly over 7 cm long and about 5 cm wide, submerged leaves narrow-linear, often absent
Broad-leaved Pondweed *(Potamogeton natans)*

Floating leaves up to 7 cm long and about 3 cm wide (not always present). Submerged leaves narrowly lance-shaped
Various-leaved Pondweed *(Potamogeton gramineus)*

8 Floating leaves with kidney-shaped lobes, submerged ones dissected
Water-Crowfoot *(Ranunculus aquatilis)*

Floating leaves rhombic, forming a mosaic-like rosette on the water surface
Water Chestnut *(Trapa natans)*

9 Leaves floating on water in a rosette, circular, heart-shaped at the base
Frog-bit *(Hydrocharis morsus-ranae)*

Leaves not as above 10
10 Leaves oval, arranged in two opposite rows
Water Fern *(Salvinia natans)*

Leaves or shoots not as above 11
11 Shoots covered with small, egg-shaped scale-like leaves
Fairy Moss *(Azolla filiculoides)*

Shoots not as above 12

12 Plants shaped like small roundish discs
Duckweed *(Lemna)*, *(Wolffia)*

Leaves forked
Crystalwort *(Riciella)*

Submerged plants

Plants living submerged under water

1	Plants with a more or less wide leaf-blade	2
	Plants with awl-shaped or greatly dissected leaf-blade	14
2	Leaf margin with distinct spines	13
	Leaf margin not as above	3
3	Leaves alternate or opposite	4
	not as above	10
4	Leaves with wavy margin, linear elongate	

     Curly Pondweed *(Potamogeton crispus)*

	Leaves smooth	5
5	Leaves clasping the stem	

     Perfoliate Pondweed *(Potamogeton perfoliatus)*

	Leaves not clasping the stem	6
6	Leaves large, elliptical, tapering	

     Shiny Pondweed *(Potamogeton lucens)*

	Leaves not as above	7
7	Leaves linear, ribbon-shaped	8
	Leaves small, inversely egg-shaped to linear or spatula-shaped	9
8	Leaves up to 21 cm long and 3–4 mm broad	

     Grass-wrack Pondweed *(Potamogeton compressus)*

Leaves up to 8.5 cm long, 2–3 mm broad

     Grassy Pondweed *(Potamogeton obtusifolius)*

9   Leaves inversely egg-shaped to linear, opposite, the ends of the shoots frequently on the water surface, with the leaves bunched into a rosette

     Water Starwort *(Callitriche)*

Leaves spatula-shaped, opposite on stem. Plantlets form low, turf-like stands

     Waterwort *(Elatine)*

10 Leaves arranged in 3 ranks on stem, sharply keeled, broad egg-lance-shaped, tapering

     Willow Moss *(Fontinalis antipyretica)*

Leaves not arranged in 3 ranks on stem 11
11 Leaves 3 in a whorl, elongate, rounded at tip

    Canadian Pondweed *(Elodea canadensis)*

Leaves not arranged as above 12
12 Leaves in basal rosette, linear

    Water Lobelia *(Lobelia dortmanna)*

Leaves or plantlet lance-shaped, on one side narrowing into a stalk, bearing a root on the underside

    Ivy Duckweed *(Lemna trisulca)*

13 Leaves in funnel-shaped rosette, up to 40 cm long, margin with spinous teeth

    Water Soldier *(Stratiotes aloides)*

Leaves in close groups of 3, mostly linear, shallow-lobed with spinous teeth

    Najas

14 Leaves alternate 15
    Leaves differently arranged on stem or basal 18
15 Leaves narrowly linear, clasping the stem with a large green sheath

    Fennel-leaved Pondweed *(Potamogeton pectinatus)*

Leaves many times forked 16
16 Leaves with small bladders at the tip

    Bladderwort *(Utricularia)*

Leaves not as above 17
17 When removed from water leaves collapse, like a paint brush; many times forked, 7–16 cm long

    Long-leaved Water-Crowfoot *(Ranunculus fluitans)*

When removed from water leaves rigidly spread out, sessile, much shorter than stem internodes

    Stiff-leaved Water-Crowfoot *(Ranunculus circinatus)*

18 Leaves whorled 19
    Leaves not whorled 21
19 Leaves comb-like segmented

    Water-milfoil *(Myriophyllum)*

29

Leaves not as above
20 Leaves coarse, with spines, once or twice bristly, forked

Hornwort *(Ceratophyllum)*

Leaf-like lateral branches at the nodes with short outgrowths or forked in the upper parts

Stoneworts *(Chara* and *Nitella)*

21 Leaves comb-like segmented

Water Violet *(Hottonia palustris)*

Leaves awl-shaped   22
22 Leaves very fine, bristle-like, four-sided compressed

Slender Spike-rush *(Eleocharis acicularis)*

Leaves coarsely awl-shaped   23
23 Leaves rush-like, arranged spirally on a compressed axis

Quillwort *(Isoetes lacustris)*

Leaves 4–10, the outer ones cylindrical, the inner ones more oval in cross section

Shore-weed *(Littorella uniflora)*

DESCRIPTIONS OF WATER PLANTS

Emergent Plants

Horsetail, *Equisetum*

The horsetails are cryptogams (spore-bearing plants) of a character-istic structure. A rhizome creeping in the soil gives rise to erect stems which are mostly annual. At the nodes between the long internodes there are sheaths, with many teeth, and closed all round; they take the place of leaves. The surface of the internodes is usually grooved. The lateral branches are vertical, divided into hollow internodes and arranged in whorls.

Habitat

Wet soil, margins of lakes and ponds, river banks for both species.

Marsh Horsetail, *Equisetum palustre* L.
Water Horsetail, *Equisetum fluviatile* L.

The Water Horsetail grows in water up to a depth of 1 m, while the Marsh Horsetail usually occurs only on swampy soil.

Botanical Features

The **Marsh Horsetail** is 20–60 cm high. The stems bearing the sporangia are similar to the vegetative ones and appear at the same time. The stem is rather soft, grass green, simply branched, grooved, some-what rough, about 3 mm in diameter, with a narrow central cavity. The sheaths are loose-lying, cylindrical-bell-shaped, with 6–10 lance-shaped teeth with broad, white margin.

The **Water Horsetail** grows up to 1.5 m in height; fertile and sterile stems are also similar in appearance. They are mostly unbranched, occasionally slightly branched at the top. They are about 8 mm in diameter, with a wide central cavity. The stem is striped. The sheaths usually have 10–13 teeth which are awl-shaped, blackish-brown and have a narrow white margin.

Importance for fishing and economic value

In loose stands the Water Horsetail is rather useful since fish like to shelter there. But if it develops in dense, turf–like stands the water cannot warm up and light penetration is hindered.

It is difficult to eradicate. It is said to be susceptible to potassium fertilizer.

31

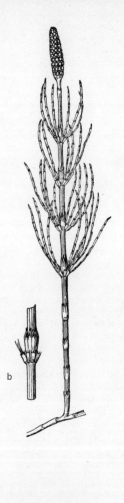

Water Horsetail
Equisetum fluviatile L.
$1/6$th nat. size
a internode with sheath

Marsh Horsetail
Equisetum palustre L.
$1/3$rd nat. size
b internode with sheath

Reedmace, *Typha*

Habitat

On margins of lakes and river banks, in ponds, marshes and meadow bogs, forming extensive stands.

The Lesser Reedmace produces conspicuous, large stands in the deeper regions of ponds.

Botanical Features

A perennial creeping rhizome up to $2^1/_2$ cm in diameter, soft, rich in starch, edible. The leaves are up to 2 m long, with long sheaths; they stand rigidly erect, are arranged in two rows and narrowly linear. A layer of mucilage is secreted by the sheath; this prevents water entering the stem and leaf sheath. The male and female flowers form cylindrical spikes. The upper spike is purely male, the lower one female. The male flowers consist of 3 stamens, anthers on a short stalk which has a crown of hairs projecting at the base; the female ones have an ovary with a similar long style. Wind pollination. Flowers July–August. Reproduction mainly by shoots arising from rhizome.

There are two different species of Reedmace:

Great Reedmace *(Typha latifolia* L.*)* leaves up to $2^1/_2$ cm broad, bluish-green. The male and female spikes are contiguous. Flowers without bracts. The ripe spike is blackish-brown.

Lesser Reedmace *(Typha angustifolia* L.*)* differs from the last species mainly by the narrower leaves, only up to 1 cm wide and grass-green, and the narrower spikes in which a piece of stem, 3–5 cm long, separates the male and female parts. The ripe female spike is a reddish cinnamon colour. The female flowers are in the axils of brachts which are as long as the hairs, but much shorter than the stigmas.

Importance for fishing and economic value

Reedmace is the plant which contributes most to the process of silting. As in the reed its hard, large leaves decompose only very slowly, forming unproductive cellulose detritus. The dense, extensive system of rhizome makes a firm network. In ponds the luxuriant growth of reedmace may become disastrous if the bottom has not been worked for a few years. Then the dense stands of reedmace resemble a luscious field of corn. In general the Lesser Reedmace is less common. Both species are usually found as pure and extensive stands.

The leaves contain many fibres; they are used for plaiting, in cooperage for caulking of barrels, and in recent times, for the manufacture of cardboard. The leaf fibre can be used for ropes and textiles, but it is very brittle.

33

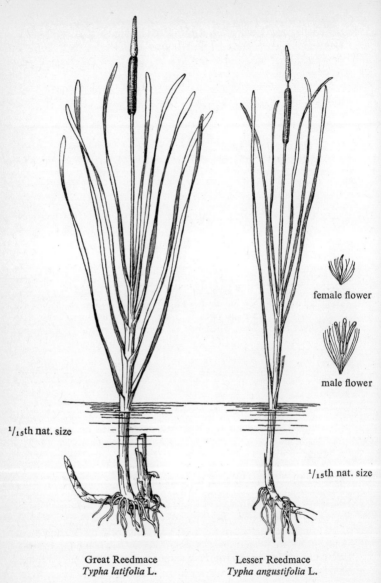

female flower

male flower

$^1/_{15}$th nat. size

$^1/_{15}$th nat. size

Great Reedmace
Typha latifolia L.

Lesser Reedmace
Typha angustifolia L.

34

In order to keep reedmace down it must be cut several times a year (see reed p. 42). As far as possible cutting should be done immediately above ground; in this way most shoots are struck, even those about to develop. The water penetrating into the cut surface causes the plants to die.

Bur-reed, *Sparganium erectum* L. (Syn: *S.ramosum* Hudson)

Habitat

In the marginal zone of lakes and ponds, preferably in muddy ground, frequently with reedmace and reed; it often forms large clumps in the marginal zone.

Botanical Features

The tuberous rhizome develops from the end of a runner bent upwards; on the underside it bears scales and above them a rosette of leaves, triangular in section, sword-shaped towards the top, 1–2.5 cm wide, and up to 1.5 m long. The inflorescence is always much shorter than the basal leaves; it is branched and there are conspicuous leaves at the base of the flowering branches. At the bottom of the stronger branches there are 2–4 globular female flower heads and above them 10–20 male ones. The female flowers consist of 3 wedge-shaped petals and one ovary, the male ones of 3 small petals and 3 stamens. The plant is wind pollinated. The ripe fruit resembles a rolled-up hedgehog.

Importance for fishing

The Bur-reed is a plant of muddy situations; when occurring in dense stands it casts shade on the water and may make production of fish food difficult.

Unbranched Bur-reed, *Sparganium emersum* Rehm

Habitat

Far less common than *Sparganium erectum*, but is found also in the silted zones of stagnant or flowing water.

Botanical Features

In contrast to the Bur-reed, the inflorescence is unbranched, bearing only 2–5 female and up to 8 male flower heads. The plant is 20–70 cm high, somewhat longer when floating. The leaves are distinctly keeled, triangular at the base and narrower than those of the Bur-reed. Flowers June and July.

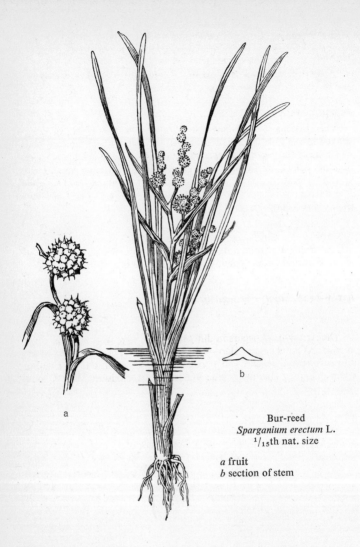

Bur-reed
Sparganium erectum L.
$^1/_{15}$th nat. size

a fruit
b section of stem

Importance for fishing

Being less common it is of less importance to fishing than the Bur-reed.

36

Water Plantain, *Alisma plantago-aquatica* L. (Syn: *A plantago* L.)

Habitat

Associated with emergent plants. In muddy bays of lakes, in marshes and ditches. Often in large masses in ponds.

Botanical Features

The rhizome is thickened into a tuber. The spoon-shaped, long-stalked leaves form a basal rosette. All leaves may bear axillary buds which serve for vegetative reproduction. Ribbon-shaped aquatic leaves develop before the aerial ones. The pyramidal flower spike, with spreading branches and flower stalks, bears white or reddish-white flowers; they consist of 3 sepals and 3 petals, 6 stamens and 15–30 carpels. Flowers June–October.

Importance for fishing

The Water Plantain occurs in muddy situations and is a binder of mud; as such it is not welcome, especially in large numbers.

Arrow-head, *Sagittaria sagittifolia* L.

Habitat

The Arrow-head occurs in different forms, especially when growing in mud. As an emergent plant it is associated with others of that zone; it may spread extensively in ponds. At greater depth and in running water only long floating, ribbon-like leaves are produced. These plants remain sterile.

Botanical Features

The Arrow-head overwinters by means of walnut-sized tubers which are rich in starch and are edible; they are produced at the end of subterranean runners and are detached in the autumn. The tubers sprout in spring, first producing a few ribbon-shaped aquatic leaves, followed by some long-stalked floating leaves and finally by the typical arrow-shaped aerial ones. The terminal, 3-angled flower stem has whorls of 3, bearing the white female flowers below; above are the male flowers, with longer stalks, opening later. Both have three dullish-red sepals and three large white petals, with a large purple patch at the base. In the centre of the female flowers there is a head of numerous carpels, in the centre of the male ones a head of numerous stamens. Flowers June–July. In deep, especially in running water only ribbon-shaped submerged leaves are produced.

Unbranched Bur-reed
Sparganium emersum Rehm
$^1/_6$th nat. size

Water Plantain
Alisma plantago-aquatica L.
$^1/_5$th nat. size

Importance for fishing

In lakes and ponds the Arrow-head indicates the presence of banks of detritus. On the whole it is of no special importance for fishing.

Arrow-head
Sagittaria sagittifolia L.
$^1/_{15}$th nat. size

Flowering Rush
Butomus umbellatus L.
$^1/_7$th nat. size

Flowering Rush, *Butomus umbellatus* L.

Habitat

The Flowering Rush is associated with the zone of emergent plants, usually solitary among other plants of the marginal zone. It is often found in the lower parts of the littoral zone of lakes in front of reedmace and reed.

Botanical Features

Perennial, with a short rhizome. Leaves over 1 m long, up to 1 cm broad, sheathed at the base, triangular, at the top pointed in a sword-shape. In the axils of the leaves there are either shoots or flower stalks, up to 150 cm high, leafless, round in cross section, in a large umbel. The conspicuous, reddish-white flowers are hermaphrodite, have 6 perianth segments, 9 dark red stamens and 6 dark red carpels joined at the base.

Importance for fishing

The Flowering Rush lives in mud, but owing to its isolated occurrence it is of little importance to fishing.

Reed-grass, *Phalaris arundinacea* L.

Habitat

Grows in wet places along rivers, in ditches, canals, streams, lakes and ponds; occasionally it forms almost pure stands. The Reed-grass does not grow in the water, but on the margin, provided there is sufficient moisture. It is completely resistant to flooding, even of long duration.

Botanical Features

A perennial grass, 0.5–2 m high very similar to Reed; it has creeping underground rhizomes. The ligule is membraneous, mostly finely dissected, but not hairy as in the reed. The spike is large, tufted, widely spreading when flowering, pale green to reddish. The spikes are unisexual. It differs from the reed by the axis of the spikelets not being hairy.

Importance to fishing and economic value

The Reed-grass is a bulky grass and on the continent it is used for bedding and as fodder. It reaches maximum development in its second year. There are two, sometimes even three harvests. Cutting is carried out as early as possible as the plant soon becomes woody. It likes fairly light soil and good manuring. It cannot stand grazing. It is well suited to strengthen dykes and banks of ditches.

Reed-grass, *Phalaris arundinacea* L.
$^{1}/_{10}$th nat. size
a inflorescence; *b* single flower

Reed, *Phragmites communis* Trinius

Habitat

The swamp zone of lakes and rivers, and in marshes and ditches. Extensive stands, usually near the margin, and growing in depths of up to 1.5 m of water. Widespread.

Botanical Features

Reed is a true grass. It is the characteristic plant of the emergent zone and a perennial, 1–4 m high; depending on the substratum it may be low-growing and sparse or tall and luxuriant on soils rich in nutrients. The subterranean creeping rhizome may be up to $2^1/_2$ cm in diameter; it is richly branched and spreads over wide areas. As in all grasses the stem has great bending strength and has nodes at certain intervals.

Leaves attached to the stem by means of a loose sheath so that, like a weather-vane, they all point the same way in the wind. As the leaves cannot tolerate flooding for any length of time and die off, the reed is a good indicator of water level.

The ligule is divided into a ring of fine hairs. This ring of hairs at the end of the sheath prevents water entering between the stem and the sheath. The spike is large, turned a little to one side and bears many flowers. The spikelets, 6–9 mm long, have 3–7 flowers. When the flowers open the glumes spread apart, exposing the long white hairs of the axis of the spikelets, making the dark purple spike appear a glistening white. Flowers August–September. Fruits ripen only in January, and occur very rarely. Widespread dispersal through asexual reproduction by means of shoots from the rootstock. There is a special way of dispersal by means of decumbent shoots. These are shoots above ground which may grow up to 10 m along the surface of the water, producing shoots and roots at the nodes.

Importance for fishing and economic value

The Reed is one of the most effective plants in causing silting. Its hard leaves and stems decompose very slowly and form the unproductive cellulose detritus. Counter measures consist in cutting several times under water, as close as possible above the bottom, for the first time when the plants have just risen above the water surface. If there is only one cutting it should be undertaken when the plants are at their greatest vigour, that is when the inflorescences begin to form. The plants can also be kept down by cattle. Many organisms are attached to the underwater parts of the Reed. Loose stands provide welcome shelter to fish. Reed has many practical uses: as material for thatching and building, as reed mats, and the young plants are used as fodder.

42

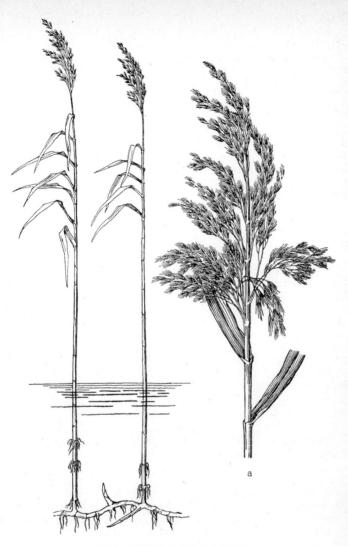

Reed, *Phragmites communis* Trinius
$1/20$th nat. size
a inflorescence

43

Scolochloa festucacea Link

Habitat

Not native to Britain. Occurs on the banks of rivers and shores of lakes in North Germany, but rare. It is often associated with stands of Reed-grass *(Glyceria maxima)*.

Botanical Features

Creeping rhizome. Plants up to 2 m high, lateral branches usually non-flowering. Leaves deep green, broadly linear, gradually tapering. Flowering spike spread out, overhanging at tip, branched, very loose. Spikelets with 3–4 flowers.

Importance for fishing

Scolochloa has excellent properties which would make it advisable to introduce it generally into fishing waters. The large soft leaves make it a suitable fodder grass. It has been recommended for the protection of dams.

Reed-grass, or Great Water Grass, *Glyceria maxima* (Hartm) Holmb. (Syn: **G.aquatica** [L.] Whlnb.)

Habitat

Abundant at the margins of fresh and brackish waters in lowland areas. It is remarkable for the luxuriant development of its leaves. It often occurs in rafts of vegetation.

Botanical Features

The Great Water Grass is a true grass; up to 2 m high, perennial, yellowish-green. Rhizome creeps extensively, stem usually erect. Leaves cutting, about 1.5 cm wide, keeled at the back. Flowering spike very large (20–40 cm), much branched, tufted. Spikelets usually with 5–8 flowers, 8 mm long, light green, in the end brownish or with a purple tinge. Flowers July–August.

Importance for fishing

The Great Water Grass provides emergent vegetation readily sought after by fish; but it sometimes grows in such dense patches that it casts heavy shadow on the water; therefore it is not popular with people managing the water. In ponds of medium depth it often grows in turf-like formation. As the Great Water Grass is softer than reed and reed-mace it decomposes more rapidly and is less troublesome.

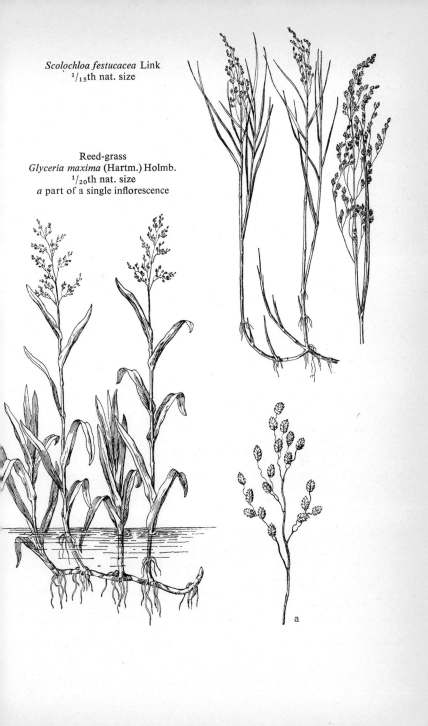

Scolochloa festucacea Link
$\frac{1}{15}$th nat. size

Reed-grass
Glyceria maxima (Hartm.) Holmb.
$\frac{1}{20}$th nat. size
a part of a single inflorescence

a

Flote-grass, *Glyceria fluitans* (L.) R. Br.

Habitat

Flote-grass is mainly found in stagnant or slow-flowing water, in ditches and wet meadows. Unlike the Great Water Grass it does not form dense emergent stands.

Botanical Features

The plant is perennial, 40–120 cm high, with a creeping rhizome. Its weak stems and leaves bend on all sides to the water surface or float in shallow water. Leaves flat, with linear keels, up to 8 mm wide. Spike very long (up to 50 cm), narrow, turning to one side. Before and after flowering the branches are adpressed; during flowering they project at right angles. Spikelets up to 2 cm long, with 7–11 flowers. Anthers violet. Fruit 3 mm long. Flowers June–September.

Importance in fishing and economic value

Flote-grass is a useful plant of the banks. Insect larvae and other small animals shelter under the floating leaves lying loosely on the water. The seeds have been used for human food ('manna groats').

Bulrush, *Schoenoplectus lacustris* (L.) Palla (Syn. *Scirpus lacustris* L.)

Habitat

The stands of Bulrush usually form the inner boundary of the emergent vegetation, and penetrate more deeply into the water than any other plants of that zone. They grow in large beds in lakes, ponds and slow-flowing water.

Botanical Features

The Bulrush (often wrongly called 'Rush') belongs to the family of Cyperaceae (the Cyperaceae are not grasses in the true sense of the word, although they often resemble grasses). It is perennial with a strong, slow-growing rhizome which creeps on the soil surface. The dark green, cylindrical stems reach up 3 m in length and a diameter of up to $1^1/_2$ cm; they are erect and leafless; only at the base there are a few leaves, 10–40 cm long with a very long sheath and a rudiment of a linear leaf-blade. The inflorescence is a terminal spikelet; the spikelets are unequally stalked and bear many flowers. The bract is no longer, or even shorter, than the inflorescence. The flowers are found in the axils of oval, reddish-brown bracteoles; there are 6 bristle-like perianth segments, 3 stamens and a superior ovary with a long style and 3 awl-shaped stigmas. Fruit triangular, nearly 3 mm long, remains of style persisting.

46

Flote-grass, *Glyceria fluitans* (L.) R. Br.
$^1/_{12}$th nat. size
a part of a single inflorescence

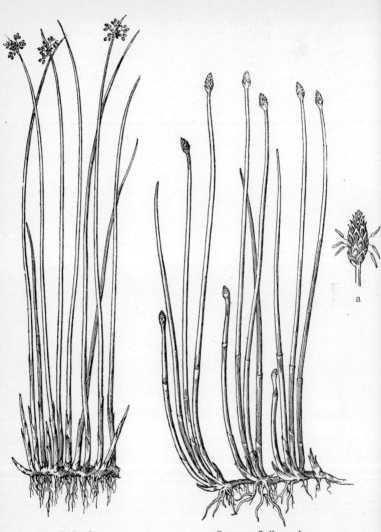

a

Bulrush
Schoenoplectus lacustris (L.) Palla
$^1/_{20}$ th nat. size

Common Spike-rush
Eleocharis palustris (L.) Roem & Schult
$^1/_2$ nat. size
a spikelet

48

Importance for fishing and economic value

The bulrush is one of the worst plants to produce silting and one of the most troublesome binders of mud. In the zone of emergent vegetation it provides little cover and little food. The stems are filled with pith and resemble cork in their buoyancy; they can be used for eel bobs and floats. But the Glaucous Bulrush, *S. tabernaemontani* (Gmelin) Palla, is preferable as it is stronger and absorbs less water. The Glaucous Bulrush occurs only locally. The Bulrush is used for woven goods (plaiting).

As a plant causing silting it should be eradicated. It can be said to be the most resistant water plant; this is specially evident in ponds.

Common Spike-rush, *Eleocharis palustris* (L.) Roem & Schult

Habitat

Common on shallow banks of ditches, marshes, etc.

Botanical Features

The Common Spike-rush also belongs to the family Cyperaceae. It is perennial, has a rhizome, and the stem resembles that of rushes. Height 15–50 cm. The inflorescence is a brown terminal spike. Flowers June–August.

Importance for fishing

The thread-like rhizomes form a firm cover which prevents erosion of sandy banks and provides fish with warm spawning places and abundant food. The plant fulfils a useful function in fishing waters and is therefore welcome.

Sedges, *Carex* L.

Habitat

Sedges prefer marshy, acid soils. They are marsh plants rather than aquatics, but grow well in shallow water.

Botanical Features

Sedges are members of the Cyperaceae and are a widespread genus with many species. They are perennials with a rhizome. Their leaves are linear, narrow and cutting, the flower stalks sharply triangular. Flowers in cylindrical, brownish spikes, singly or in groups; male and female flowers either together in one spike or separately on different ones.

49

Tufted Sedge, *Carex acuta* L.

Rhizome with creeping runners. Plants 40–100 cm high. Leaf-blade 5–10 mm wide. Stem acutely triangular. Spikelets slender, cylindrical, female spikes 2–4, male ones about 3. The bract of the lowest spikelet greatly overtopping the stem. Fruit elongate, shortly beaked, 4–5 veins on either side. 2 stigmas.

Cyperus Sedge, *Carex pseudocyperus* L.

Plant light green, tufted, up to 1 m high. Stem acutely triangular, very rough at top. A terminal male spike; 3–6 female spikes long-stalked, compact, pendulous. Fruit spindle-shaped, projecting, gradually tapering into long, bifid beak. 3 stigmas.

Beaked Sedge, *Carex rostrata* Stokes

Plant up to 60 cm high. Stem bluntly triangular, shorter than leaves. Sheaths net-veined. Male spikes 2–3, female ones 3–5. Bracts exceeding inflorescence. Fruit almost spherical with short, two-teethed beak. 3 stigmas.

Great Pond-sedge, *Carex riparia* Curtis

Plant up to 150 cm high. Stem acutely triangular. Leaf-blade with deep midrib. Male spikes 2–6, female ones 2–5. Bracts reddish-brown, hair-like tips. Fruit elongate, with two-teethed beak. 3 stigmas.

Importance for fishing and economic value

Sedges are plants which cause silting. They often occur in hillocks: dense accumulations of the leaves and flower stalks which are gradually compacted downwards to a column-like formation bearing on top a tuft of green leaves and flower stalks.

If sedges occur in ponds they indicate poor conditions for fishing.

Bog Arum, *Calla palustris* L.

Habitat

An introduced plant which is naturalized in some places: wet woods, near ponds, etc.

Botanical Features

Calla palustris has a long creeping rhizome. Height 15–50 cm. The long-stalked leaves are roundish, heart-shaped, pointed, firm and

50

Tufted Sedge *Carex acuta* L.
¹/₆th nat. size

leathery. The spadix, about $2^1/_2$ cm long, has inconspicuous hermaphrodite flowers (the uppermost flowers are sometimes male only); below it is the elliptical spathe, green on the outside and white inside. Flowers June–July. Fruits scarlet berries. The plant is poisonous.

Sweet Flag, *Acorus calamus* L.

Habitat

Margins of lakes and ponds, usually confined to rather shallow water. Often occurring in considerable numbers.

Botanical Features

Perennial plant, rhizome thickness of a finger. The leaves are sword-shaped, resembling a sheath at the base, smooth, glossy, fresh green, easily recognisable by the crinkling of one edge. The inflorescence with its inconspicuous greenish flowers appears to be lateral as the green spathe, resembling a leaf, takes up a position continuous with the flattened stem. Ripe red fruits are never found here. Reproduction only by means of rhizomatic shoots. The plant originated in East Asia and was naturalized in England by 1660. When bruised the Sweet Flag has an aromatic scent.

Importance for fishing and economic value

Sweet Flag is responsible for silting to some extent, but never forms extensive stands like the reed and reedmace. It is not harmful to water management. Its aromatic and bitter rhizomes have been used medicinally in stomach, intestinal and liver complaints, anaemia, gout and inflammation of the gums.

Rushes, *Juncus*

Habitat

Rushes prefer very damp, mostly wet banks where they grow in groups.

Botanical Features

Rushes are perennials with a compact rhizome. Some form clumps, others loose turf. They belong to the family of Cyperaceae. Leaves and flower stalks are round in cross section. The leaves are surrounded by some scales at the base. In the species described the inflorescence appears to be on one side as the sheath forms an apparent continuation of the stem. The Rushes are wind pollinated.

52

Bog Arum, *Calla palustris* L.
$^1/_3$rd nat. size

Sweet Flag, *Acorus calamus* L.
$^1/_{10}$th nat. size

53

Soft Rush, *Juncus effusus* L.

Will grow up to 80 cm. Leaves and stem are cylindrical, dark green, glossy and the pith is continuous. Soft Rush has a loose inflorescence distinctly lateral; it consists of many individual stalked flowers. The flowers have 3 stamens. Flowering begins in June. The fruit is a capsule, inversely egg-shaped, three-sided, depressed at the tip. The style sits in a depression. Forms clumps.

Conglomerate Rush, *Juncus conglomeratus* L.

30–60 cm high, differs from the last species by its spherical inflorescence condensed into a ball and its leaves of a dull greyish green; the pith is continuous. The fruit is reddish-brown, blunt at the tip, ending with the remains of the style resting on a small elevation. Flowering begins in May. Forms clumps.

Hard Rush, *Juncus inflexus* L. (Syn. J. *glaucus* Sibth)

Height 30–60 cm. Leaves and stem are bluish green, with prominent ridges and dull. The pith is interrupted. The basal leaf sheaths are dark brown and glossy. The inflorescence closely resembles that of the Soft Rush; in the latter it appears round the stem while it is somewhat flattened in the Hard Rush. The flowers have 6 stamens. Flowers from June. Capsule blunt, with a spiny tip. Forms clumps.

Importance for fishing and economic value

As long as the plants form loose stands in the water they are not undesirable as fish like to spawn among them. Rushes are of no value as fodder, but have been used for animal bedding as they are highly absorbent.

Yellow Flag, *Iris pseudacorus* L.

Associated with other emergent plants, in ditches and marshes.

Botanical Features

The Yellow Flag, 60–100 cm high, is a perennial. It has a thick, branched rhizome and sword-shaped leaves, about 2 cm broad, arranged in two ranks. The inflorescence has only a few flowers. The large yellow flowers have 6 perianth segments of different shape; those of the outer ring are large deflexed (bent outwards) with a dark yellow brown-veined honey guide; the three smaller ones of the inner ring are erect. 3 stamens. Ovary three-chambered, inferior. Fruit a conspicuous capsule. Flowers May and June.

54

Yellow Flag, *Iris pseudacorus* L.
$^1/_{10}$th nat. size   *a* flower

Conglomerate Rush *Juncus conglomeratus* L.
$^1/_3$rd nat. size

55

Great Water Dock, *Rumex hydrolaphatum* Hudson

Habitat

Margin of lakes, ponds, singly in ditches.

Botanical Features

Among the emergent vegetation the Great Water Dock is conspicuous by its very large leaves. The perennial plant grows up to 2 m and is slightly branched. The leaves are broadly lance-shaped, the lower ones 40–100 cm long, stalked and with a slightly wavy margin. The inner tips of the fruit perianth segments are egg-shaped triangular, margin entire or toothed at the base; in the centre there is an elliptical tubercle. Flowers June–August. Rare in the north.

Water-pepper, *Polygonum hydropiper* L.

Habitat

Shallow water and damp places.

Botanical Features

Water-pepper is an annual plant. The leaves are lance-shaped, tapering at either end; they have a peppery, mordant taste. The spikes are loose, slender, thread-like. The inconspicuous green flowers have a pinkish tinge at the tip and have 6 stamens. Flowers July–September.

Marsh Marigold, Kingcup, *Caltha palustris* L.

Habitat

Marshy meadows, margins of streams and ditches.

Botanical Features

Plants 15–30 cm high, with stout rhizome. The lower leaves are long-stalked, the upper ones sessile. Leaf-blade roundish, deeply heart-shaped at the base, leaf margin crenate. Flower with 5 petaloid yellow sepals, numerous stamens and 5–8 free carpels. Flowers April–June. Of no importance for fishing.

Great Spearwort, *Ranunculus lingua* L.

Habitat

Widespread, usually singly in flat country, associated with emergent vegetation; also in ditches.

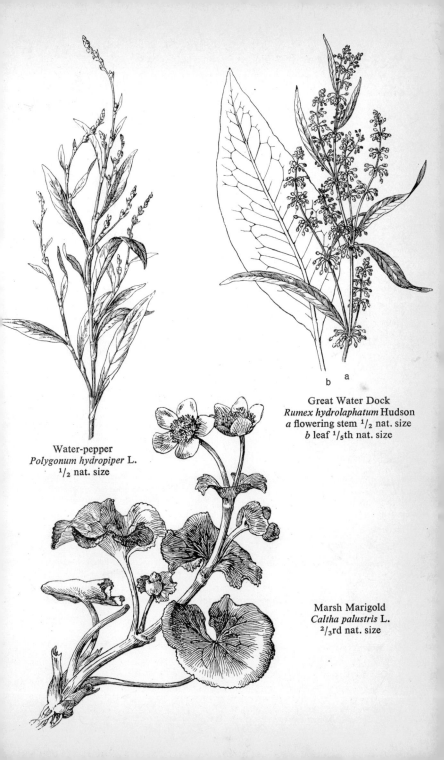

Water-pepper
Polygonum hydropiper L.
$^1/_2$ nat. size

Great Water Dock
Rumex hydrolaphatum Hudson
a flowering stem $^1/_2$ nat. size
b leaf $^1/_5$th nat. size

Marsh Marigold
Caltha palustris L.
$^2/_3$rd nat. size

Great Spearwort
Ranunculus lingua L.
$1/_{10}$th nat. size

Botanical Features

Plants up to 1.5 m high, stiffly erect, perennial. Non-flowering shoots with long-stalked, heart-shaped leaves; flowering specimens have short-stalked leaves, narrow to linear-lance-shaped, pointed, entire margin; lower leaves sometimes remotely toothed. Large, golden-yellow flowers. Flowers June—August.

58

Great Yellow-cress
Rorippa amphibia
(L.) Bess
$^1/_2$ nat. size

Great Yellow-cress, *Rorippa amphibia* (L.) Bess

Habitat

Associated with emergent plants in shallow parts of still or slow-flowing water.

Botanical Features

The Great Yellow-cress is perennial, growing to 1 m or more. The rhizome creeps horizontally in the ground. The ascending stem is usually several times branched. Leaf shape very variable. The lower leaves may be lyre-shaped to comb-like pinnate or else broadly lance-shaped and undivided. They taper into a small stalk, mostly without auricles. The

59

Water-cress,
Rorippa nasturtium-aquaticum (L.) Hay
$^2/_3$rd nat. size

upper leaves are sessile, lance-shaped, tapering into the leaf base which is usually without auricles. The margin may be entire, irregularly dissected, toothed or crenate. The small golden-yellow flowers of the Cruciferae type have inflorescences with many flowers in corymbs. Flowers May–August.

Water-cress *Rorippa nasturtium-aquaticum* (L.) Hay, (Syn: *Nasturtium officinale* R. Br.)

Habitat

In springs, streams, rivers and ditches with pure water; usually in groups forming dense small masses.

Botanical Features

The main root soon disappears and is replaced by a horizontal rhizome with adventitious roots. The plant becomes erect, rising from its procumbent position and grows up to 1 m high. The stems are

60

angular, hollow and hairless. The leaves are pinnate, the lower ones stalked, with 1–3 leaflets, the upper ones 5–8 segments; at the base they have short horizontal auricles, are grass green and somewhat fleshy. The unpaired terminal roundish or heart-shaped leaflet is considerably larger than the very shallow lobed elliptical lateral leaflets. The small flowers, of the Cruciferae type, have white petals and yellow anthers. The fruits are usually sickle-shaped and about as long as the stalk. In rather deep running water the plants live completely submerged, forming luxuriant masses and overwintering green. The leaves are slightly larger. The completely submerged plants do not flower.

Importance for fishing and economic value

The water-cress is well liked especially in trout streams. Many animals on which the fish feed are found between the plants. It is also important as food; its aromatic, slightly bitter leaves are eaten as salad. In medicine it is used to purify blood, settling the stomach, stimulating metabolism and preventing catarrh.

Purple Loosestrife, *Lythrum salicaria* L.

Habitat

Common in lakes and ponds, associated with emergent vegetation.

Botanical Features

Purple Loosestrife is a perennial. It grows to 1 m or more. The stem is angular, simple or slightly branched. The sessile leaves are broadly lance-shaped, tapering, opposite or in whorls of three. The reddish-purple flowers, in the axils of leaf-like bracts, are terminal in long spikes. The calyx is cup-shaped, with triangular teeth at the end and 6 teeth on the outer calyx. The 6 petals are oblong elliptical, blunt. Flowers July–September.

Mare's-tail, *Hippuris vulgaris* L.

Habitat

At margins of still or slow-flowing water as well as in deep stagnant water. According to locality may be emergent, half submerged, or completely submerged. It prefers cool, calcareous water. Grows in patches.

Botanical Features

Perennial, with creeping rhizome. It resembles a horsetail in appearance, but is a flowering plant, not a spore-bearing one. The narrowly-linear, dark green leaves are arranged in whorls of many parts; above water they are stiffly horizontal, while drooping under water. The in-

61

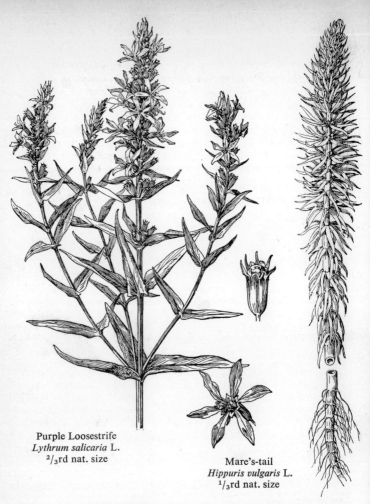

Purple Loosestrife
Lythrum salicaria L.
²/₃rd nat. size

Mare's-tail
Hippuris vulgaris L.
¹/₃rd nat. size

conspicuous hermaphrodite flowers are found in the axils of the aerial leaves; they consist of one stamen and one pistil. Flowers July–August. Typically Mare's-tail is half submerged. In water up to 80 cm depth half the plant—or four-fifths—is under water, with typical submerged leaves, while the part rising above the water bears aerial leaves and flowers. The terrestrial form does not usually exceed 20 cm while the submerged form may be 1.5 m long. It may occur in water as deep as 4 m, but it does not flower and its leaves are particularly large and numerous.

Importance for fishing

Because of its softness the Mare's-tail may be considered useful in fishing waters.

Large Bitter-cress, *Cardamine amara* L.

Habitat

Moist places in woods, in springs and ditches, mostly in patches.

Botanical Features

The Large Bitter-cress closely resembles the Great Yellow-cress. It is chiefly distinguished from it by the pithy stem which is usually slightly hairy in its lower part; the flowers are somewhat larger and the anthers are purple. Flowers April–May.

Of no importance for fishing.

The leaves have an aromatic, somewhat bitter taste, and on the continent are sold as 'water-cress'.

Large Bitter-cress
Cardamine amara L.
$^1/_2$ nat. size

Cowbane, *Cicuta virosa* L.

Habitat

Shallow places among emergent vegetation. Very local in East Anglia, N. Ireland and E. Scotland.

Botanical Features

Plant very poisonous. The rhizome is tuberous, hollow and septate, with an aromatic scent. The stem is 1–1.5 m high, tubular and finely ridged. The leaves are vividly green, large, three-pinnate with tapering

63

Cowbane
Cicuta virosa L.
$1/2$ nat. size
a section through rhizome

tips, more or less saw-edged. The umbel usually has no bract; the bracteoles consist of many leaves. Main umbel 8–18 rays. Flower of the general Umbelliferae type. Flowers July–August.

Water-parsnip, *Sium latifolium* L.

Habitat

Usually singly in shallow parts among old emergent vegetation, in ditches, marshes and still water. Local.

64

Water-parsnip
Sium latifolium L.
$^1/_2$ nat. size
a cross section of stem
b part of a single leaf-stem

a   b

Botanical Features

A perennial about 1.2 m high. The stem is angular and ribbed. The rhizome produces runners and is covered with thick root hairs. Leaves simply pinnate, oblong-lance-shaped, sharply saw-edged, with an uneven leafbase. Submerged leaves are dissected and 2-pinnate. The umbels have many flowers without marginal ray-florets. The main umbel is clearly terminal; the numerous bracteoles have entire margins. Flowers July–August.

65

Narrow-leaved Water-parsnip, *Berula erecta* (Huds.) Coville. (Syn. *Sium erectum* Hudson)

Habitat

In and around ditches, streams, springs and ponds. Emergent and submerged, usually in water 15–80 cm deep. Often in groups; mainly in flat country.

Botanical Features

Plant up to 60 cm high, with thin, creeping rhizome. Stem roundish, striate, hollow. The leaves are simply-pinnate, the basal ones much elongated, with 7–9 pairs of sessile, inversely egg-shaped, narrow leaflets. The stem leaves are lance-shaped, singly or doubly sharply crenate. The umbels are short-stalked, the first ones being considerably overtopped by the subsequent ones. Bract and bracteoles many-leaved, partly segmented. The best known form is half submerged. The submerged form has no flowers and often develops turf-like stands which, unless frozen up, overwinter. Flowers July–August.

Importance for fishing

The Narrow-leaved Water-parsnip is valuable in fishing. In small runnels it is an effective coarse filter. In trout streams it gives welcome shelter to trout. The submerged leaves act like those of the valuable submerged plants.

Fine-leaved Water Dropwort, *Oenanthe aquatica* (L.) Poiret

Habitat

In ponds, ditches, marshes and associated with emergent vegetation in slow and still water. Local.

Botanical Features

The Fine-leaved Water Dropwort is an annual or biennial which dies off after fruits have ripened once. The rhizome is turnip-shaped. The stem is erect, round in cross section, hollow, striate and mostly much branched. The leaves are 2–3 pinnate and triangular in outline. Submerged leaves divided into many hair-like segments. The leaflets of the aerial leaves are egg-shaped in outline, deeply dissected, the tips lance-shaped with entire margin. The umbel of the main axis is overtopped by those of the lateral axes. Bracts absent or a few only; when present they are, as the numerous bracteoles, awl-shaped, with entire margin. Flowers June–August. The plant reproduces by means of runners and seeds.

66

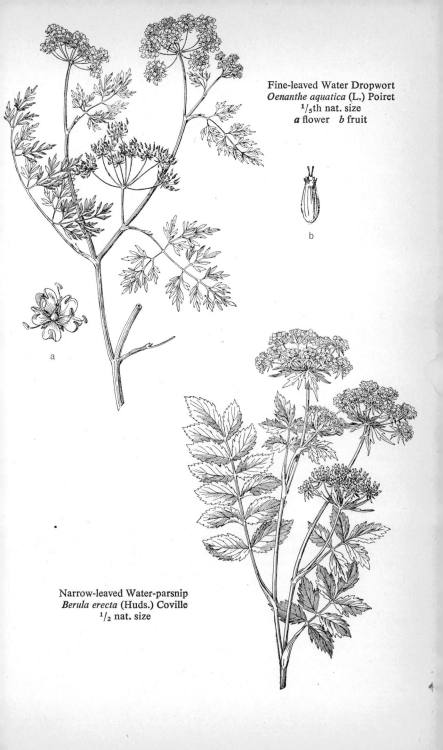

Fine-leaved Water Dropwort
Oenanthe aquatica (L.) Poiret
$^1/_5$th nat. size
a flower   *b* fruit

b

a

Narrow-leaved Water-parsnip
Berula erecta (Huds.) Coville
$^1/_2$ nat. size

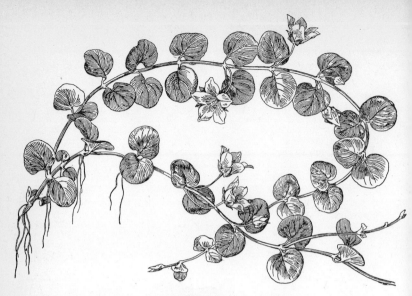

Creeping Jenny, *Lysimachia nummularia* L. $^1/_2$ nat. size

The Fine-leaved Water Dropwort is suspected of being poisonous. Medicinally it was used for asthma, bronchitis, pulmonary complaints, mucous flow from the kidneys and bladder, etc.

Creeping Jenny, *Lysimachia nummularia* L.

Habitat

Wet meadows, in and around ponds, ditches and pools.

Botanical Features

Creeping Jenny is a perennial, with trailing stems and occurs both on land and in the water. The terrestrial form creeps on the ground while the shoots of the submerged one are usually erect. The stem is 4-angled. Roots develop at the nodes of the stem. The first leaves are broadly spatula-shaped to egg-shaped, and short-stalked. The submerged shoots bear almost exclusively this type of leaf. The emergent leaves are more or less egg-shaped, the leaf-blade is coarser and darker green than in the submerged leaves. The leaf-stalk is about 3–7 mm. The yellow flowers of the terrestrial form are found in the leaf axils. Their stalk is about as long as the leaves. Flowers May–July.

Creeping Jenny is of no special significance in fishing as it does not normally form large stands in the water. It is often used in coldwater aquaria, but it will keep for only a few months. It is a valuable plant in a vivarium. *Lysimachia nummularia* may also be grown in hanging baskets.

Tufted Loosestrife, *Naumburgia thyrsiflora* (L.) Reichenbach (Syn. *Lysimachia thyrsiflora* L.)

Habitat

In shallow water of the banks of lakes and fens in the north; rare elsewhere.

Botanical Features

A perennial plant, erect, unbranched. It grows to about 70 cm. The leaves are lance-shaped, tapering, margin entire; they are in crossed pairs (decussate) base mostly clasping the stem. The small flowers have golden-yellow, linear petals; they are arranged in dense axillary racemes. Flowers June–July.

Yellow Loosestrife, *Lysimachia vulgaris* L.

Habitat

Widespread in fens and beside rivers and lakes, but rarer in the north.

Botanical Features

A perennial plant, up to 1.5 m high. Leaves usually in whorls of three, broadly lanceolate, tapering, margin entire, short-stalked. The golden-yellow flowers are in 5 parts, in terminal spikes which bear leaves at the base. Flowers June–August.

Bogbean, *Menyanthes trifoliata* L.

Habitat

Edges of lakes, ponds and in the wetter areas of bogs and fens.

Botanical Features

The plant grows to about 30 cm and has a rhizome up to 125 cm long which creeps on the ground or in the mud. The leaves are in 3 parts, clover-like, long-stalked; they clasp the rhizome with a long sheath. The flower stalk is 25–40 cm high, ending in a rather dense spike. The

Tufted Loosestrife
Naumburgia thyrsiflora (L.) Reichenbach
$^{1}/_{2}$ nat. size

Yellow Loosestrife
Lysimachia vulgaris L.
$^{1}/_{5}$ th nat. size

Bogbean *Menyanthes trifoliata* L.
$^1/_2$ nat. size

flowers are white with pink outside; 5 petals fringed inside. Flowers May–June.

Of no importance for fishing. The plant was used medicinally for weak stomach, neuralgia, etc.

Water Forget-me-not, *Myosotis scorpioides* L.

Habitat

Shallow banks of still and slow-flowing water, on marshy meadows, in ditches and ponds.

Botanical Features

The Water Forget-me-not has a creeping rhizome. Its angular stem is prostrate in its lower part and erect in the upper one. The stem leaves

71

Water Forget-me-not
Myosotis scorpiodes L.
$^1/_2$ nat. size

are alternate, oblong, blunt at the top, tapering into the stalk below, with short rough hairs. The vividly light blue flowers are in loose cymes. Flowers May–July, and usually again later on.

Common Skull-cap, *Scutellaria galericulata* L.

Habitat

Plant on banks of margins of lakes, ponds, rivers and ditches.

72

Common Skull-cap
Scutellaria galericulata L.
$^1/_2$ nat. size

Botanical Features

The Skull-cap is perennial; it usually grows erect, frequently branched and up to about 40 cm high. The opposite leaves are very short-stalked. The leaf-blade is lance-shaped, cordate at the base, the leaf margin crenate. The blue-violet flowers of the Labiatae type are single and one-sided in the leaf axils. Flowers June–September.

73

Marsh Woundwort
Stachys palustris L.
nat. size

Marsh Woundwort, *Stachys palustris* L.

Habitat

Often associated with emergent vegetation.

Botanical Features

Perennial with underground rhizome. Mostly unbranched, 70 to 140 cm high. The stem is 4-angled, leaves in crossed pairs, broadly lance-shaped, tapering somewhat heart-shaped at the base, saw-edged, with soft hairs. The reddish-purple flowers—of the Labiatae type—form false whorls in the axils of leaf-like bracts; they form a spike 5–20 cm long. Flowers June–September.

74

Importance for fishing and economic value

As the plant forms no extensive stands it is of no special significance for fishing. It should be mentioned that, particularly towards the autumn, segments of the rhizome produce tuberous swellings which are edible (like potatoes). These tubers, 5–11 cm thick, are relished by pigs.

Gipsy-wort
Lycopus europaeus L.
$^1/_2$ nat. size

Gipsy-wort, *Lycopus europaeus* L.

Habitat

Widespread on the banks of still and slow-running water.

Botanical Features

Perennial, up to 1 m high and branching. Leaf shape varies from a leaf-blade divided into comb-like segments and those where the margin is coarsely toothed. Transitional forms are pinnate in the lower parts and coarsely toothed in the upper ones. The small white flowers—of the Labiatae type—are arranged in dense whorls in the leaf axils. Flowers July–August.

75

Water Mint
Mentha aquatica L.
$^1/_2$ nat. size
a submerged form

Water Mint, *Mentha aquatica* L.

Habitat

Among emergent vegetation, in marshes and ditches, also alongside
running water. Sterile, non-flowering forms occur to a depth of 2 m.

Botanical Features

The Water Mint has a rather thin rhizome with long segments. It
attains 60–100 cm. The stalked leaves are egg-shaped, saw-edged, hairy
and in crossed pairs. The flower whorls are compressed into a terminal,
globular head. Below this there are often a few, poorly developed flower
whorls in the leaf axils. Flower of the Labiatae type. Flowers July–
August. Of no special importance for fishing.
Medicinal uses: stomach and intestinal complaints, migraine and other
troubles.

76

Woody Nightshade
Solanum dulcamara L.
$^1/_2$ nat. size

Bittersweet, Woody Nightshade, *Solanum dulcamara* L.

Habitat

On banks of lakes and rivers, but not in the water. Frequently in hedges, woods and on waste ground.

Botanical Features

The plant has a rhizome creeping in the ground. It may be prostrate, or climb between other plants of the bank. The leaf shape very variable: usually egg-shaped, lance-shaped, also spear-shaped or with two narrow lobes at the base. The flowers have petal-like corolla lobes and are of a striking purple, with a central column of 5 golden-yellow anthers. The egg-shaped berries are bright red. All parts are poisonous. Flowers June–September.

Of no importance for fishing.

77

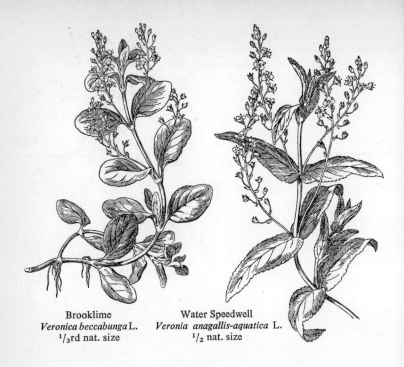

Brooklime
Veronica beccabunga L.
$^1/_3$rd nat. size

Water Speedwell
Veronia anagallis-aquatica L.
$^1/_2$ nat. size

Brooklime, *Veronica beccabunga* L.

Habitat

In streams, ditches and springs, mostly half-submerged.

Botanical Features

30–60 cm high, with creeping rhizome. Stem fleshy cylindrical, hollow. Leaves short-stalked, elliptical, blunt, crenate-saw-edged. Flowers blue, in loose racemes. Flowers May–September. The under-water form overwinters green.

Importance for fishing

Specially valued in trout streams.

Water Speedwell, *Veronica anagallis-aquatica* L.

Habitat

As last species.

15–50 cm high. Leaves sessile, half clasping the stem, egg-lance-shaped, pointed, slightly saw-edged. Flowers pale blue, with reddish-violet veins, racemes with many flowers. Flowers June–October.

Importance for fishing

The plant is valued in trout streams and their tributaries.

Trifid Bur-marigold, *Bidens tripartita* L.

Habitat

Scrub on banks, margins of ponds, in general in marshy places.

a

Trifid Bur-marigold
Bidens tripartita L.
$1/2$ nat. size *a* fruit

Botanical Features

The Trifid Bur-marigold is an annual, 50–100 cm high, with branched, purplish-red stem. Leaves mostly three-lobed, opposite, tips saw-edged. The flower-heads, $1^1/_2$–$2^1/_2$ cm in diameter, are brownish-yellow, erect, solitary in leaf axils. Bracts in two ranks, the outer ones green, resembling leaves, the inner ones oval, brownish-yellow. Ray florets mostly absent. Disc florets brownish-yellow, hermaphrodite. Fruits flattened, with a barbed bristle at each of the top corners, 2 awns. Flowers July–October.

Importance for fishing

With their barbed bristles the fruits may get caught in the fishes' gills, causing festering wounds. In order to avoid such injuries the plant should be cut before fruits have formed.

Nodding Bur-marigold, *Bidens cernua* L. has thicker stems, unstalked, undivided leaves, nodding flower-heads, and narrower fruits with 3–4 barbed bristles.

79

Floating-leaved Plants

Floating Crystalwort, *Riciella fluitans* L.

Habitat

Pools in woods and bogs as well as ponds; sometimes on wet mud.

Botanical Features

Floating Crystalwort belongs to the liverworts. On damp muddy soil it produces star-shaped, small rosettes which are anchored in the soil with a few rhizoids. In the water the small plants elongate, are several times forked and distinctly flattened. The aquatic form has few or no rhizoids. As the plants contain wide air spaces they float on the water surface, frequently forming a dense cover.

Importance for fishing

In places where the Floating Crystalwort occurs in such numbers as to produce a dense cover it cuts the light off from the water and must be considered harmful to fishing. It blocks fishing gear and makes it more difficult to clean and dry. The aquarist values the plant as a producer of oxygen.

Water Fern, *Salvinia natans* Allioni

Habitat

Although native to warmer regions of the continent this plant disappeared from the British Isles in the Ice Age. This and related species are, however, popular in tropical aquariums in this country and may occasionally find their way into natural waters.

Botanical Features

Salvinia natans, a fern, is an annual. It floats freely on the water surface. The axis can attain 20 cm and be slightly branched. A whorl of three consists of two oval small floating fronds and one tufted, colourless aquatic frond which grows vertically into the water, and takes on the function of the root. The spherical sporangia are found at the base of the floating fronds.

Fairy Moss, *Azolla filiculoides* Lam.

Habitat

Introduced from North America and naturalized in several places in Europe. In still and slow-flowing water; mainly in Southern England.

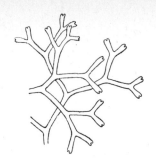

Floating Crystalwort,
Riciella fluitans L.
2 ×nat size

Fairy Moss,
Azolla filiculoides Lam.
2 ×nat. size

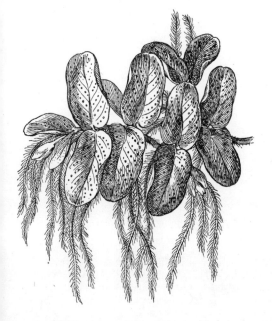

Water Fern, *Salvinia natans* Allioni 2 × nat. size (from Lehrbuch der Botanik)
a from the side, with round sporocarps, × submerged leaves

81

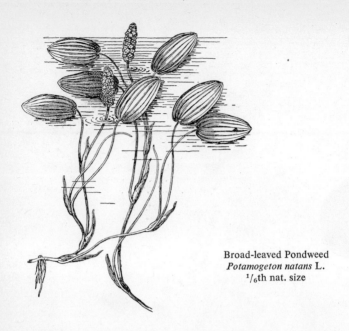

Broad-leaved Pondweed
Potamogeton natans L.
$^1/_6$th nat. size

Botanical Features

The stems of this small fern are up to 1–5 cm long, pinnately branched and have egg-shaped, scaly leaflets. Fine rhizoids hang into the water. Sporangium spherical. The plants turn reddish in autumn.

Broad-leaved Pondweed, *Potamogeton natans* L.

Habitat

In lakes and ponds; preferably in still, more rarely in running water.

Botanical Features

The Broad-leaved Pondweed is a perennial with a long, branched rhizome and two kinds of leaves. The lowest, submerged ones, are round in cross section, without leaf-blade, decaying at an early stage, mostly dead at flowering time. The floating leaves are coarse, leathery, oval or oblong. Stipules may reach 10 cm, often longer than leaf-stalk. The stalks of the spike are not thickened upwards. The spike has many flowers. Flowers June–August.

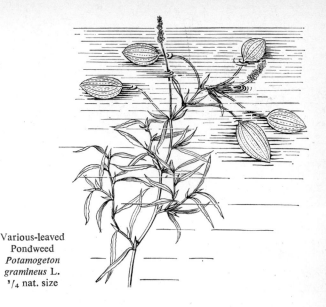

Various-leaved
Pondweed
*Potamogeton
gramineus* L.
$^1/_4$ nat. size

Importance for fishing

Leaves and stem are richly colonized by all kinds of animals and the
floating leaves lie loosely on the surface, but if too dense they can prevent light reaching the water. As a plant of rich organic silt it is not
popular on fishing waters.

Various-leaved Pondweed, *Potamogeton gramineus* L.

Habitat

Locally common in lakes, ponds, streams and canals, especially
where the water is acid.

Botanical Features

A thin, strongly forked rhizome anchors the Various-leaved Pondweed to the bottom of the water. It may grow over 1 m and produces
two types of leaves. The submerged ones are narrow, lance-shaped,
4–6 cm long and about 8 mm wide, translucent, sessile; the floating
leaves are egg-shaped-elliptical (not always present), leathery, up to

83

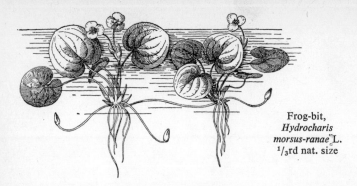

Frog-bit,
*Hydrocharis
morsus-ranae* L.
$^1/_3$rd nat. size

7 cm long and 3 cm wide, stalked. Stipules at least on the submerged leaves. Spikes about 3 cm long, frequently in closely adjoining pairs. The fruits have a blunt keel at the back and a short tip. Flowers June–August.

Frog-bit, *Hydrocharis morsus-ranae* L.

Habitat

A floating plant, local in ponds, ditches and canals in the south and in Ireland.

Botanical Features

The Frog-bit is a non-rooting floating plant, absorbing nutrients from the water through its unbranched aquatic roots. The floating leaves are about 4 cm in diameter, round, heart-shaped at the base, arcuate, parallel-veined; they rest on the water in a rosette. Stolons arise in the leaf axils; their ends produce new rosettes from which further stolons are formed. As all connecting stolons survive the summer extensive stands result. In the autumn the last-formed stolons terminate in winter buds, $1–1^1/_2$ cm long, elongate, egg-shaped and rich in starch. These detach themselves and sink to the bottom; the following spring they become lighter and rise to the surface to grow into new plants. The white flowers are unisexual, the male ones mostly in threes, the female ones singly in an inflorescence. In many places only one sex is found so that no fertile seeds can be produced; only asexual reproduction ensures the maintenance of the species.

Importance for fishing

The underside of the leaves is usually densely colonized by animals on which fish feed and by snail spawn. The plants can be tolerated in fishing waters provided they do not form a continuous cover.

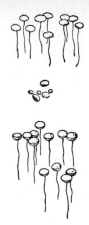
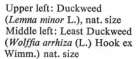
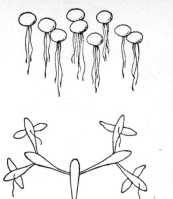

Upper left: Duckweed
(*Lemna minor* L.), nat. size
Middle left: Least Duckweed
(*Wolffia arrhiza* (L.) Hook ex
Wimm.) nat. size
Lower left: Gibbous Duckweed
(*Lemna gibba* L.), nat. size

Upper right: Great Duckweed
(*Lemna polyrrhiza* L.),
nat. size
Lower right: Ivy Duckweed
(*Lemna trisulca* L.),
nat. size

Duckweeds, *Lemna, Wolffia*

Habitat

Quiet waters and bays, especially in farm and village ponds, frequently in large masses.

Botanical Features

Small floating plants consisting of a leaf-like thallus bearing on its underside one or several rootlets—or none at all. Reproduction almost exclusively asexual by means of budding. Flowers are unisexual; the male ones consist of 1 anther, the female ones of 1 pistil; but they occur only rarely. The duckweeds overwinter at the bottom of the water with their stomata closed.

1. Duckweed, *Lemna minor* L.

is the most widespread form. Thalli round or egg-shaped, mostly 2–3 mm in diameter, flat, dark green above, lighter below. One root arises on the underside.

85

2. Great Duckweed, *Lemna polyrrhiza* L.

about 5–8 mm in diameter, flat, green above, reddish on underside, with a bundle of roots.

3. Gibbous Duckweed, *Lemna gibba* L.

somewhat larger than *Lemna minor*. Round or egg-shaped, thallus 3–5 mm swollen beneath, with one root.

4. Ivy Duckweed, *Lemna trisulca* L.

Completely submerged; only floating on surface during flowering. Lance-shaped, tapering at base into a stalk, with a root on the underside. Usually several thalli joined together by their stalks.

5. Least Duckweed, *Wolffia arrhiza* (L.) Hook. ex Wimm.

This smallest flowering plant has a diameter of only 1–1.5 mm. No flowers have been observed in Britain. Thalli are slightly swollen above, more so beneath; there are no roots. This little plant is very local in the south; it usually occurs together with other duckweeds.

Importance for fishing

If duckweeds occur in large masses they cast heavy shadow and prevent the water warming up. They make oxygen exchange more difficult and promote the production of detritus. They are very troublesome when netting, since they block the meshes. In ponds receiving farm effluents a plant cover, 1 cm thick, may form every day.

Amphibious Bistort, *Polygonum amphibium* L.

Habitat

A plant highly adaptable to varying environmental conditions. It occurs in stagnant and slow-flowing water and is specially suitable for ponds which are drained in winter or waters with a frequently changing water level since it grows equally well in water and on dry ground.

Botanical Features

The plant overwinters with a creeping rhizome, and flowers from June–September. It occurs in two forms: the aquatic one has a stem about 1 m long, floating, containing air spaces; it has long-stalked floating leaves (the leaf-stalk arising above the middle of a papery sheath), bluntly tapering at the top, glossy, dark green, leathery. The terrestrial form has erect shoots, the leaves are narrower, their stalks shorter, soft and with stiff hairs. The inflorescence is compact, cylindrical. The pink flowers have 5 petals and 2 stigmas.

86

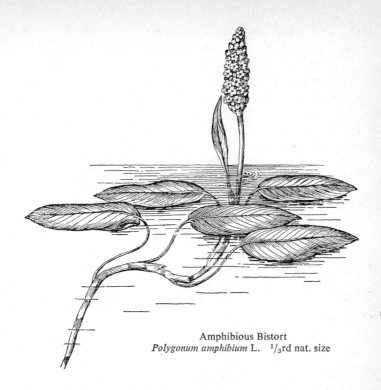

Amphibious Bistort
Polygonum amphibium L. $^1/_3$rd nat. size

Importance for fishing

The stems and leaves of the Amphibious Bistort provide shelter and food for many animals on which fish feed. The floating leaves are usually loosely spread on the water surface so that illumination is not impeded. It is a welcome plant in fishing waters. Its great adaptability to varying environmental conditions makes it specially suitable for waters which are drained in winter.

White Water-lily, *Nymphaea alba* L.

Habitat

In lakes, ponds and canals to a depth of about 1.5 m rarely deeper. It is characteristic of the zone of floating-leaved plants.

87

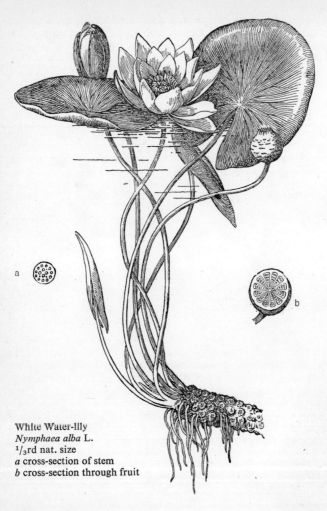

White Water-lily
Nymphaea alba L.
$1/3$rd nat. size
a cross-section of stem
b cross-section through fruit

Botanical Features

The rhizome is very stout and has roots and leaf scars all round. It grows to over 1 m in length. Cabbage-like underwater leaves are produced far more rarely than in the Yellow Water-lily. The floating leaves are long-stalked, very large, leathery, with two lance-shaped stipules;

88

they are round with a deep, narrow dent at the base. The leaf-stalk is round in cross section. The flowers, mostly 9–12 cm in diameter, have 4 (rarely 5) green sepals on the outside. The petals are white, spirally arranged and there is a gradual transition into the numerous anthers. The stigma is plate-shaped and usually has 8–24 radiating stigmas. The fruit is spherical. Flowers June–August.

Importance for fishing and economic value

These following remarks apply in general both to the White and the Yellow Water-lily. Their leaves often cover the water surface completely, thus preventing illumination, even movement of water so that aeration becomes impossible. The thick rhizome contributes in a great measure to silting. Though the Water-lily is an ornament for the water, the fisherman must keep a watchful eye on it. The rhizome is used as pig food in some countries but in some areas the plant is completely protected.

Yellow Water-lily, *Nuphar lutea* (L.) Smith

Habitat

In stagnant or slow-flowing water, in places which are sheltered from the wind. Up to 2 m in depth, generally in slightly deeper water than the White Water-lily, often dominant in the zone of floating-leaved plants.

Botanical Features

The rhizome is very stout (up to 10 cm) and may reach a length of 3 m; it bears knobbly leaf scars on its upper side, and on its underside numerous adventitious roots. At the tip of the rhizome thin, light green, cabbage-like submerged leaves develop at first, followed by the long-stalked oval floating leaves, heart-shaped at the base, and leathery. Near the leaf margin the lateral veins fork in an acute angle, while in the White Water-lily the angle is less acute and branching more net-like; in addition there are more lateral veins in the Yellow Water-lily. Under unfavourable conditions only submerged leaves are produced. The stems contain many wide air spaces and are roughly triangular in cross section. The long-stalked flowers are solitary and have 5 yellow sepals. The numerous spatula-shaped yellow petals are only $^1/_3$ the length of the sepals. The numerous stamens are shorter than the pistil. The fruit is green, flask-shaped and on ripening it breaks up into several white, spongy lamellae containing the seeds. Flowers June–August.

Importance for fishing and economic value

With its thick, branched rhizome the Yellow Water-lily contributes to silting to a large extent. If gases of decay form underneath, the plants

a

Yellow Water-lily, *Nuphar lutea* (L.) Smith. ¹/₃rd nat. size
a cross-section of stem

Water-Crowfoot
Ranunculus aquatilis L.
$^2/_3$rd nat. size

rise; the roots take important nutrients from the bottom. The floating leaves often form a practically continuous cover on the surface so that light cannot reach the water. Only the soft submerged leaves add oxygen to the water and are useful.

Water-Crowfoots, *Ranunculus* spp.

These widely distributed plants can easily be recognized in general by their finely divided lower leaves and lobed floating leaves and also by their showy white flowers. There are several species somewhat difficult to separate except in broad groups, and a general description must suffice here.

Water-Crowfoot, *Ranunculus aquatilis* L.

Habitat

Mainly in stagnant water, ponds, lakes, etc., but also in slow-flowing water, often covering large areas.

Botanical Features

The Water Crowfoots overwinter with parts of the floating stems sticking in the mud; there are two kinds of leaves. The floating leaves are kidney-shaped, mostly 3–5 pinnate. The submerged leaves are finely dissected, repeatedly 3-pinnate, lastly forked. When removed from the water they collapse like a paint brush. There are the most varied transitional forms between floating and submerged leaves. The flowers arise in a position opposite the origin of the leaves; they rise above the surface, are solitary, about $2-2^1/_2$ cm broad and have 5 petals and 5 white sepals with yellow honey-guide at the bottom. The many stamens are somewhat longer than the stigma. Flowers June–August. Fruitlets oval, rounded above and rough-haired at the tip, with a small, laterally displaced remnant of the style.

Importance for fishing

The stands of Water-Crowfoot are well liked by fish as many animals on which they feed are found between the plants. They also have many organisms attached to them.

Water Chestnut, *Trapa natans* L.

Habitat

Occurs wild in central and southern Europe where, however, it is declining, but is not found in Britain, except as an introduced plant to garden pools.

Botanical Features

The Water Chestnut is an annual. The typical fruit has 4 spikes and edible seeds. From it floating stems with lax, linear, aquatic leaves develop in spring. Paired large feathery roots occur at the stem nodes. The stems end in a rosette of floating leaves covering the water like a mosaic. The floating leaves are leathery, stalked, with a rhombic, toothed leaf-blade. After flowering, the middle parts of the leaf-stalks swell like bladders. Flowers July–September. Flowers singly in the leaf axils, with 4 white petals, 4 stamens and a style with a capitate (head-like) stigma.

Water Chestnut
Trapa natans L.
$^1/_4$ nat. size
a fruit

Fringed Water-lily, *Nymphoides peltata* (Gmel.) O.Kuntze (Syn:
Lymnantheum nymphaeoides Link.)

Habitat

In stagnant and slow-flowing water.

Botanical Features

The rhizome is thin, creeping, branched. Adventitious roots develop
at the nodes. In spring the floating leaves with their thin, long stalks
and the inflorescences arise from the tip of the rhizome. The floating
leaves are round to oval, up to about 13 cm long; on the underside they

Fringed Water-lily, *Nymphoides peltata* (Gmel.) O.Kuntze $^2/_3$rd nat. size

are brown and bear small tubercles. The inflorescences consist of 2–3 whorls, one above the other. Below each flowering whorl are 2 bracts resembling leaves. The yellow flowers are about 3 cm across; the corolla is funnel-shaped, with 5 deep lobes and the margins are fringed. Flowers July–August. Reproduction chiefly by means of rhizomes, but also by seeds.

Importance for fishing

As long as the floating leaves of the Fringed Water-lily are spread loosely so that illumination of the water is not impeded, the plant need not be considered troublesome.

94

Stonewort   *Nitella*
$^1/_2$ nat. size

Submerged Plants

Stoneworts, *Chara* spp. and *Nitella* spp.

Habitat

Stoneworts go to some depth in lakes. They are the main representatives of the deep water plant community. There is no upward limit. They often occur on wide, well-lit littoral zones.

The chlorine content of the water is the factor of decisive importance for the occurrence of individual species while the calcium content plays only a subordinate part. Species of *Nitella* frequently form continuous cover below the stands of *Chara*.

Botanical Features

The stoneworts are a highly developed family of Algae. Their delicate structure consists of whorls of short shoots placed at regular inter-

95

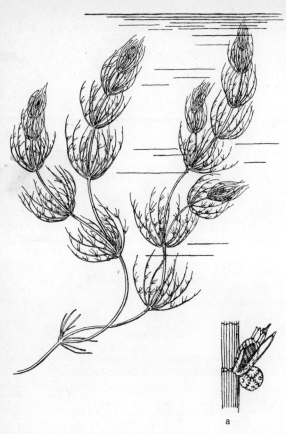

Stonewort *Chara* nat. size *a* antheridium and oogonium

vals; these are forked or bear short outgrowths, 'leaflets' at their nodes.
Cell structure and mode of reproduction reveal the stoneworts to be
Algae. At the base of the branchlets reproductive organs are found in
the summer; the female ones are green and later black; there are one
to several spherical male ones. Species of *Chara* have a cortex; those of
Nitella are without cortex. The plants are anchored in the substrate by
means of colourless rhizoids.

96

Willow Moss,
Fontinalis antipyretica L.
$^2/_3$rd nat. size

Importance for fishing and economic value

The stoneworts are valued aquatic plants. They give shelter to fish and good spawning places to some species. Many of these plants deposit large amounts of calcium on their cell walls as a result of photosynthesis. They appear covered in white, are hard to the touch and brittle. After their death dense deposits of calcium are formed in their zone. Weeded in the autumn and made into compost they provide good fertilizer.

Willow Moss, *Fontinalis antipyretica* L.

Habitat

The Willow Moss occurs in springs, streams and lakes. It is one of the chief representatives of underwater meadow deepwater plants. Owing to dependence on varying environmental conditions it displays a large variety of forms.

Botanical Features

The Willow Moss has a stem, about 50–70 cm long and grows in large, floating tufts. The leaflets are sharply keeled, broadly lance-shaped, tapering, placed in three ranks on the stem. The spore capsule formed only when the moss is stranded on wet mud is almost completely sunk in on short lateral shoots. The moss remains green in winter.

97

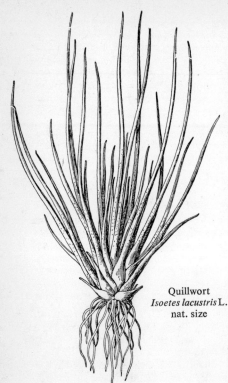

Quillwort
Isoetes lacustris L.
nat. size

The moss is well liked as shelter by animals on which fish feed. In spring waters it functions as filter and purifier. It is generally liked in fishing waters. In soft-water lakes which contain little nutritive material the plant cover formed by the moss are the most densely colonized habitats.

Quillwort,
Isoetes lacustris L.

Habitat

Locally abundant in mountain lakes and tarns in the Lake District, Wales and Scotland and a few scattered places elsewhere.

Botanical Features

Quillwort belongs to the cryptogams. The axis is short, compressed, with rush-like, cylindrical leaves spirally arranged. Plant up to 20 cm high. Leaves mostly erect. As a rule the compressed rhizome bears sterile sporophylls on the outside, in the middle zone macrosporophylls and in the central one microsporophylls. Megaspores usually yellowish and densely covered with small tubercles. Spores ripe May–July.

Importance for fishing

Quillwort shares the valuable properties of submerged plants. But it indicates lakes of little nutritive value.

Pondweeds, *Potamogeton* spp.

The genus *Potamogeton* has about 20 species. Four of these must be considered abundant: Broad-leaved Pondweed *(Potamogeton natans)*, Shining Pondweed *(Potamogeton lucens)*, Perfoliate Pondweed *(Potamogeton perfoliatus)* and Curly Pondweed *(Potamogeton crispus)*. Less common, but widespread is Fennel-leaved Pondweed *(Potamogeton pectinatus)*. (See also pages 82, 83)

The pondweeds are perennial aquatic plants. The branched creeping rhizomes occur in muddy ground. They often form a mat-like, interwoven network which may play its part in silting.

Nutrients are absorbed through roots and by the leaves.

Three different kinds of leaves may be distinguished:

1. the broad, submerged leaf, 2. the awl-shaped, grasslike aquatic leaf, and 3. the oblong-oval, leathery, long-stalked floating leaf (stomata on the upper side). According to the conditions of the locality the shape of the leaves is very variable. The leaves are in 2 ranks, mostly sessile, occasionally clasping the stem, alternate or rarely apparently opposite on the stem which is usually floating. At flowering time the inflorescences are raised above water and the inconspicuous greenish-brown flowers are wind pollinated. After fertilization the inflorescences are withdrawn into the water. Fruits usually of 4 brownish drupes or achenes. Vegetative reproduction of pondweeds takes place through broken-off branches able to produce new plants as well as by means of rhizome ends covered with scales; in addition, according to the species, through all kinds of transitional forms of winter buds.

Importance for fishing and economic value

Pondweeds offer good spawning places for young fish which like to shelter in the tangled leaves; there are plenty of attached organisms and an abundance of animals on which fish feed. The plants die off in the autumn forming organic detritus rich in nutrients. The leaves are mostly delicate and translucent casting only a moderate shadow on the bottom of lake or pond. Stems and leaves are frequently encrusted with a thick layer of calcium carbonate as the calcium bicarbonate dissolved in water is being deposited as a result of photosynthesis. Pondweeds may be used as green manure.

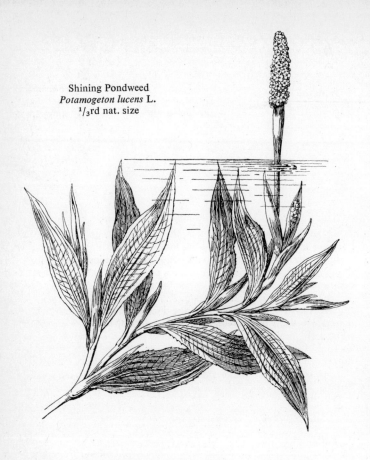

Shining Pondweed
Potamogeton lucens L.
$1/3$rd nat. size

Shining Pondweed, *Potamogeton lucens* L.

Habitat

In lakes, ponds, rivers and ditches, preferring deeper water.

Botanical Features

The plant is perennial and has a thick rhizome. The leaves are very short-stalked, large, elliptical, tapering at both ends, vivid, glossy green. The leaf shape is very variable. The stalk of the flower spike is thickened upwards. Spike with many flowers. Flowers July–August.

100

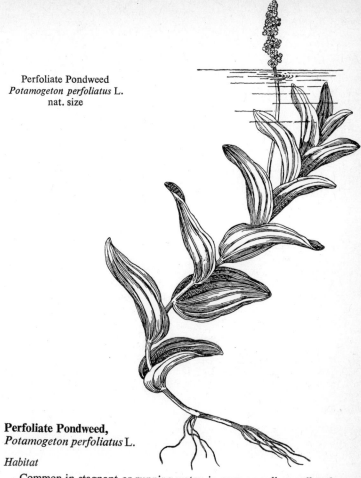

Perfoliate Pondweed
Potamogeton perfoliatus L.
nat. size

Perfoliate Pondweed,
Potamogeton perfoliatus L.

Habitat

Common in stagnant or running water, in pure as well as polluted water, usually in loose stands. Elongated shoots are produced in running water.

Botanical Features

A perennial plant with an extensively creeping rhizome. The leaves are bluntly oval, average length 2–2.5 cm and 1.3–3.5 cm wide, heart-shaped at the base and clasping the stem. Spike with many flowers, stalk not thickened upwards. Flowers July–August.

101

Curly Pondweed *Potamogeton crispus* L. ²/₃rd nat. size

Curly Pondweed, *Potamogeton crispus* L.

Habitat

Common in still and in running water.

Botanical Features

The Curly Pondweed has a very thin, richly branched rhizome. The stem is 4-angled, compressed. The leaves are linear-oblong, with undulate margin. Stem and leaves often reddish. The spikes are short, bearing few flowers. The plant produces winter buds. Flowers June–September.

Grass-wrack Pondweed
Potamogeton compressus L
$^1/_2$ nat. size

Grass-wrack Pondweed,
Potamogeton compressus L.

Habitat

Very local and mainly in the south.

Botanical Features

The Grass-wrack Pondweed has a long creeping rhizome. Its stems may reach 2 m; they are compressed and partly even more or less winged. The linear leaves, up to 20 cm long and up to 4 mm wide, are tapering at the end; they have 2 pairs of lateral veins and a spiky tip. The whitish stipule is two-keeled. The spike, about 1 cm long, bears 10–15 flowers; the flower stalks are 2–4 times as long as the spike. Flowers July–August.

103

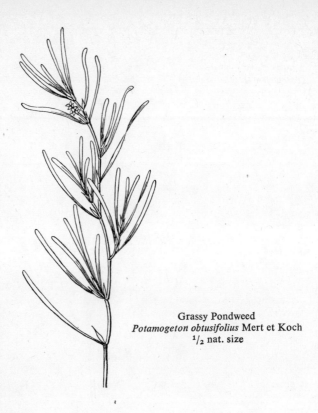

Grassy Pondweed
Potamogeton obtusifolius Mert et Koch
$^1/_2$ nat. size

Grassy Pondweed, *Potamogeton obtusifolius* Mert et Koch

Habitat

Ponds, lakes and canals; local.

Botanical Features

The Grassy Pondweed is up to 1 m long. The densely branched stems are flattened, elliptical in cross section. The linear leaves, 2–3 mm wide and up to 8.5 cm long are blunt, with a short pointed tip, usually vivid green and translucent; 3, more rarely 5 veins. The dense spike, bearing 6–8 flowers is as long as its stalk. Flowers July–August.

104

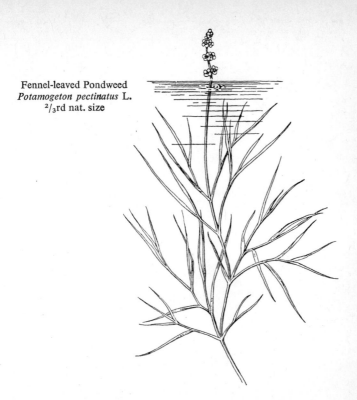

Fennel-leaved Pondweed
Potamogeton pectinatus L.
$^2/_3$rd nat. size

Fennel-leaved Pondweed, *Potamogeton pectinatus* L.

Habitat

The Fennel-leaved Pondweed occurs in still, running and even brackish water. In shallow water it usually forms fairly large stands.

Botanical Features

The stem of the Fennel-leaved Pondweed is much branched. The stipules are deciduous. The leaves are thread-like, narrowly-linear, mostly with 3 veins, with a long point; at the base a long green sheath clasping the stem. The stalks of the spike are very thin and long. The spike is interrupted, usually bearing 4–5 whorls. Flowers June–August.

105

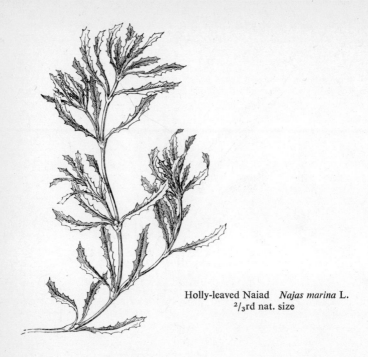

Holly-leaved Naiad   *Najas marina* L.
$^2/_3$rd nat. size

Holly-leaved Naiad, *Najas marina* L.

Habitat

Rare and confined to the Norfolk Broads.

Botanical Features

Najas marina is an annual. The stem is thin, much branched, more or less spinous (10–30 cm long); it anchors in the soil by means of adventitious roots. Leaves in close groups of three, about 2–3 mm wide and 4 cm long, mostly linear and wavy at the margin, with spinous teeth. The flowers are inconspicuous—male and female ones on different plants, but in Britain probably only female plants are found. They consist either of a single stamen, surrounded by a jug-like bract, or one pistil. *Najas* is completely adapted to aquatic life, and even pollination takes place under water. Flowering June–August.

Water Soldier
Stratiotes aloides L.
$^{1}/_{4}$ nat. size

Water Soldier, *Stratiotes aloides* L.

Habitat

In still and slow-flowing water, but local and mostly in Eastern England unless introduced. Frequently extensive meadow-like stands are formed.

Botanical Features

The leaves have a spiny, saw-edge, and are up to 40 cm long and 4 cm broad; they form a dense funnel-shaped rosette on the short main axis; below there is a dense tuft of long unbranched aquatic roots. In the leaf axils buds are produced which develop into long offsets, form leaves and aquatic roots, thus serving for vegetative reproduction. Winter buds are also produced from the leaf axils. Buds are stalked or sessile, and surrounded by a few scales. The plants have male and female flowers on different plants, but male plants are rare in Britain. Inflorescence 1 or 2 flowers, shorter than leaves. The flowers arise from a 2-leaved bract. Flower with 3 green sepals and 3 conspicuous white petals. Flowers July–August. The ripe egg-shaped fruit capsule, which is not found in Britain, projects horizontally from the 2 bracts. It often ripens without previous fertilization and is sterile. After flowering, the Water Soldier sinks to the bottom where it overwinters; it only rises to the surface in early summer, floating freely in a half-submerged state. In deeper water the plant is often permanently submerged.

Importance for fishing

Where Water Soldier has become well established it can be one of the most troublesome plants in fishing water. The animals on which fish feed live in the leaf axils and because of the spiny leaves the fish cannot get at the food. In addition, the plants which die off produce large amounts of vegetable matter which does not easily decompose, so that stretches of water where these floating masses occur are silted up after a short time.

Canadian Pondweed, *Elodea canadensis*, Michaux

Habitat

In running and quiet waters, at greater or lesser depths. Coming from North America the Canadian Pondweed was introduced into Europe in the middle of the 19th century. In the beginning it spread in such numbers that in many places navigation and fishing were obstructed.

Botanical Features

The Canadian Pondweed provides a striking example of the efficiency of asexual reproduction. In Europe only female flowers are produced and these very rarely; it multiplies exclusively by fragmentation and by winter buds. As a rule the soft, thin, branched stems bear leaves in 3 whorls; the light green leaves are sessile, oblong, rounded at the end and with a spiky tip. Leaf margins finely saw-edged.

Importance for fishing

Unless it grows in profusion the Canadian Pondweed is one of the most valuable water plants. It produces the largest amount of oxygen, thus purifying the water, and shelters large numbers of animals on which fish feed. Application of lime greatly stimulates its growth.

108

Canadian Pondweed
Elodea canadensis Michaux
nat. size

Slender Spike-rush, *Eleocharis acicularis* (L.) R. et Schult

Habitat

Rather local by ponds, ditches and marshes where it often forms large, turf-like stands.

Botanical Features

The Slender Spike-rush exists both as a terrestrial and a submerged plant. It has a creeping rhizome from which the stems arise singly or in tufts. The grass-green stems are very slender 0.2–0.6 mm in diameter, mostly 4-angled flattened; in the terrestrial form they are 4–8 cm long, in the submerged plants which are flaccid and lax up to 20 cm (rarely longer). Flowers are produced by the terrestrial plant as well as the transitional form from land to submerged plant. Flowers are borne on small egg-shaped brownish spikes at the tip of the stems.

109

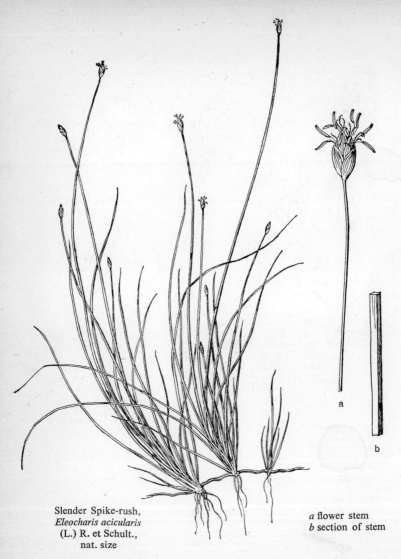

Slender Spike-rush,
Eleocharis acicularis
(L.) R. et Schult.,
nat. size

a flower stem
b section of stem

Importance for fishing

Like all soft submerged plants the Slender Spike-rush is useful in fishing especially as it covers the bottom like a carpet and presents no obstacle to fishing gear.

110

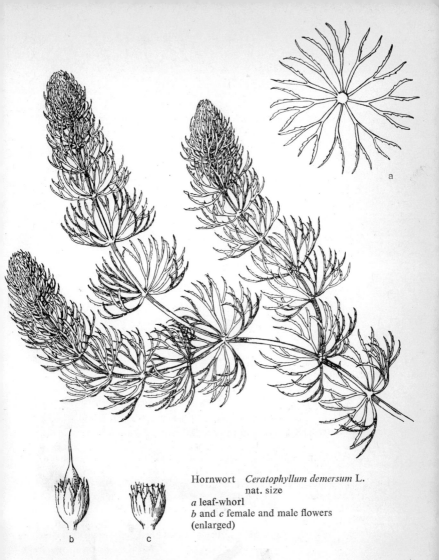

Hornwort   *Ceratophyllum demersum* L.
           nat. size

a leaf-whorl

b and *c* female and male flowers
(enlarged)

Hornwort, *Ceratophyllum demersum* L.

Habitat

Local in stagnant and slow-flowing water in England and Ireland;
rare in Wales and Scotland.

111

Botanical Features

Hornwort is a perennial plant without roots. It reaches an average length of 50–100 cm and anchors in the mud with practically colourless portions of shoot. There are many leaves in a whorl. They are rigid and brittle, with spines, bifurcating into bristly tips. Flowers develop only rarely. They are found in the leaf axils, are inconspicuous, both sexes on the same plant. Pollination takes place under water, the ripe anthers detach themselves, rise and release the pollen. Propagation almost exclusively by means of fragments of the plant and such parts of shoots whose leaves have been modified into so-called 'winter leaves'. The 'winter leaves' are divided into short terminal segments, are small, thick, and covered with thorny papillae; towards winter they form terminal buds rich in starch, which become detached from the shoot.

Importance for fishing

Hornwort has but few attached organisms and produces detritus which does not easily decompose; therefore it is of no particular value in fishing.

Spineless Hornwort, *Ceratophyllum submersum* L.

is far less common than the last species; it is distinguished from it by the leaves which fork 3–4 times, are delicate and only sparsely covered with spines.

Long-leaved Water-Crowfoot, *Ranunculus fluitans* Lamarck

Habitat

Only in running water of streams and rivers.

Botanical Features

The Long-leaved Water-Crowfoot has stems which may be several metres long; it anchors in the ground with adventitious roots arising from the stem nodes. Leaves uniform, submerged, the lower ones always longer than the internodes of the stem. The leaf-blade is divided into many straight and parallel end segments. Small, kidney-shaped, lobed floating leaves rarely develop. The flowers rise above the water surface; they are opposite the leaves and long-stalked. The flower is about 1.5–2 cm in diameter, with 5 green sepals and 4 white petals, yellow at the base. Many stamens, mostly somewhat shorter than the stigma. Flowers June–August. Fruits egg-shaped, hairless, with a short beak. Frequently no fruits are formed as permanent submergence makes fertilization impossible.

Importance for fishing

In fast-flowing water the tufts of Long-leaved Water-Crowfoot often give the only means of protection and a quiet shelter for the fish as well as providing many animals on which they feed.

112

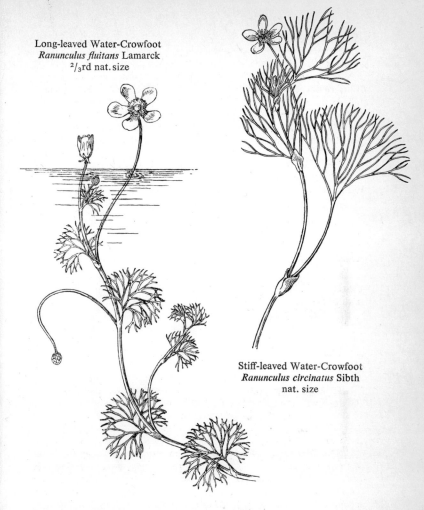

Long-leaved Water-Crowfoot
Ranunculus fluitans Lamarck
$^2/_3$rd nat. size

Stiff-leaved Water-Crowfoot
Ranunculus circinatus Sibth
nat. size

Stiff-leaved Water-Crowfoot, *Ranunculus circinatus* Sibth.

Habitat

Mainly in still water of lakes, ponds, ditches and canals, only rarely in fast-flowing water. Often in dense mass.

113

Botanical Features

Perennial. Plant 1 m or longer. The leaves are 1–2 cm long, much shorter than the internodes of the stem, tri-partite at the base, then several times forked; the outline is rounded; rigid, even after they have been removed from the water. The flowers up to 2 cm in diameter rise above the water surface. They are more or less long-stalked. Usually 5–7 petals about 10 mm long; the numerous stamens are longer than the carpels. Flowers June–August. Fruitlets up to 1.5 mm long, slightly inflated, with short bristles and ending in a short point.

Importance for fishing

Like almost all submerged plants the Stiff-leaved Water-Crowfoot is well liked in fishing waters as a producer of oxygen and because of the organisms attached to it.

Water Starworts, *Callitriche* L.

Habitat

Water Starworts are found in moderately or fast-running streams, small ponds, lakes, springs and pools. They may also occur in puddles and depressions which dry out in the warm season, but not in polluted water. *Callitriche stagnalis* also occurs in fields irrigated with sewage.

Botanical Features

Water Starworts may be divided into 2 groups: species which produce only one type of leaf *(Callitriche hermaphroditica)* and those which develop different types (primary, transitional and secondary leaves) *(Callitriche platycarpa, C. stagnalis)*. Identification of species can only be done with the help of fruits.

Autumnal Starwort, *Callitriche hermaphroditica* L. (Syn: *C. autumnalis* L.)

Local, chiefly in the north. It exists only as a submerged plant, and floating rosettes are never formed. The plants usually cover the bottom in a dense carpet. The stems are much branched, with adventitious roots in their lower parts. The leaves are opposite, linear, somewhat broader towards the base, truncated or 2-teethed at the tip; 0.4–0.7 cm long, 0.06–0.11 cm wide. Leaves always one vein only. Flowers June–autumn. Flowers, as in all species of Water Starwort, have both sexes on one plant; the male ones with 1 stamen, the female ones with 1 ovary; bracts are absent. The stigmas drop off at an early stage. The fruits are flat, circular, about 2–3 mm in diameter and have broad wings.

114

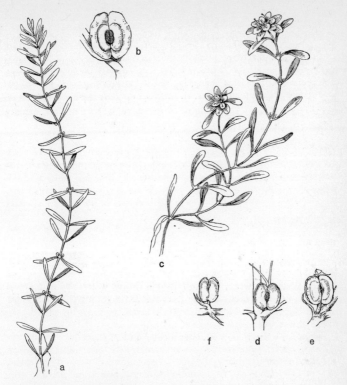

a Autumnal Starwort, *Callitriche hermaphroditica* L.   nat. size
b fruit of *C.hermaphroditica*
c *Callitriche platycarpa* Kütz nat. size
d fruit of *C.platycarpa*
e fruit of *C.stagnalis* L.
f fruit of *C.palustris* L. (*see text*)
  Illustrations after Glück

Callitriche platycarpa Kütz (Syn.: *C.polymorpha* Lönnr)

Said to be the most common species of the genus in Central Europe, *C.platycarpa* produces linear submerged leaves and transitional forms up to inversely egg-shaped floating leaves with 3 veins. Terrestrial forms have been observed, but apparently less common than in *C.stagnalis*. Flowers with bracts. Fruits 1.2–1.5 mm broad, scarcely winged or not at all, with persistent stigmas, 4–6 mm long.

115

Callitriche stagnalis Scop

Common throughout the British Isles in water and on mud up to 1000 metres. Submerged and floating leaves. Its special features are relatively large female flowers and conspicuous fruits, more or less broadly winged; at least the remnants of the styles are still projecting vertically while the fruit ripens. *C. stagnalis* may also produce terrestrial forms.

Callitriche palustris L. (Syn. C. verna L.)

British botanists consider that material from this country previously named *Callitriche palustris* and *C. verna* belongs to the species *Callitriche platycarpa* Kütz. (above) and it is doubtful if there are any authentic records of *C. palustris* L. It is said to be less branched than the other species of starwort with different kinds of leaves; often occurs in small groups or singly; has fruits 1 mm long, egg-shaped in outline, flat lobes, keeled or slightly winged; stigmas 1–2 mm long but dropping off at an early stage.

Importance for fishing

The Water Starworts are well liked in fishing waters; many animals on which fish feed occur among their leaves (including the fresh-water shrimp *Gammarus pulex* which requires much oxygen); the plants help to enrich the water with oxygen. The Starworts are particularly useful in reservoirs when these are under a cover of ice.

Waterwort, *Elatine hydropiper* L.

Habitat

Rare in pools and lakes.

Botanical Features

An annual plant forming low, cushion-like stands; it reproduces by seeds. It has a creeping stem bearing roots at the nodes; the small lateral shoots rise vertically. The leaflets are spatula-shaped, tapering at the base into a stalk, opposite. In the submerged form they attain about 16 mm, but are shorter and more compact in the terrestrial form. Large numbers of inconspicuous flowers are produced in the leaf axils.

A related species *E. hexandra* (Lapierre) DC. is slightly less rare and occurs in peaty pools and lakes. It has shorter leaves, and nearly straight seeds.

Waterwort, *Elatine hydropiper* L.   nat. size

Whorled Water-milfoil, *Myriophyllum verticillatum* L.

Habitat

In still or slow-flowing waters but not found in Scotland.

Botanical Features

There is no main root; the stem anchors the plant like a rhizome, and is only slightly branched and creeping. Leaves usually 5 in a whorl, comb-like pinnate, ending in very fine segments. Only the erect inflorescences rise above water level. The small flowers are adapted to wind pollination, usually in whorls of 6 in the axils of bracts, female ones below, male ones above. Floral bracts very variable in shape, as long as flowers or longer. The lower female flowers consist of a 4-celled ovary with 4-lobed (capitate), feathery, stigmas; the upper male ones have 8 stamens. Flowers June–August. Reproduction and overwintering

117

by means of winter buds which are formed at the end of shoots or in the leaf axils September–October; they are dark green and thickening upwards like a club. They are modified shoots with a reduced axis, 2–17 mm long and with many small tough leaves, densely arranged in whorls of 4.

Spiked Water-milfoil, *Myriophyllum spicatum* L.

Habitat

In stagnant and running water, preferably in areas rich in chalk.

Botanical Features

The Spiked Water-milfoil differs from the last species by its leaves being generally in whorls of 4, the flowers also in whorls of 4. The bracts of the lowest flowers are as long or longer than the flowers, pinnate; all others are entire and shorter than the flowers. No winter buds are produced.

Importance for fishing

The two species of Water-milfoil are submerged plants valuable for fishing. They have the largest number of attached organisms and offer good feeding places and shelter to fish. On dying off they produce detritus rich in nutrients. Being flaccid they offer no obstacle to nets.

Water Violet, *Hottonia palustris* L.

Habitat

The Water Violet prefers shallow zones of silting and muddy, slow-flowing ditch water. It likes quiet places with easy access to light.

Botanical Features

The typical form of the plant which perenniates with a rhizome is the submerged one, but reduced terrestrial forms may develop which produce no flowers. The stem is little branched and has spirally arranged, comb-like pinnate leaves. At the end of the shoots the long-stalked inflorescences rise above water; at the base they are surrounded by leaves compressed into a rosette. The pale, lilac-white flowers, are found in the axils of whorled bracts; they are either pin-eyed or thrum-eyed. After flowering the inflorescences curve downwards and the many-seeded capsules ripen in water. Flowers May–June. Overwintering by means of winter-buds (hibernacula) which are produced at the end of stolon-like branches by the leaves closing up like buds.

118

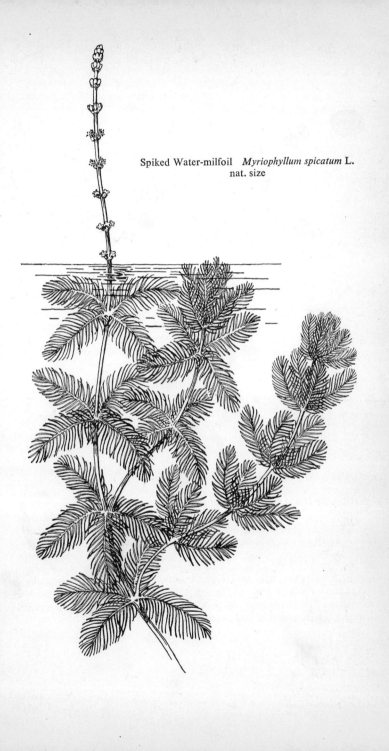

Spiked Water-milfoil   *Myriophyllum spicatum* L.
nat. size

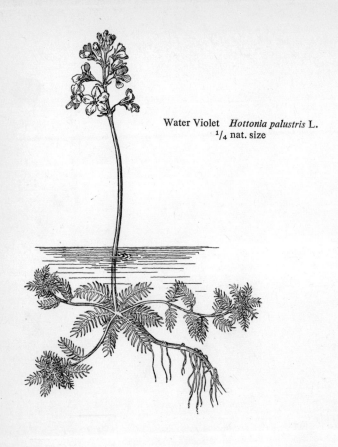

Water Violet   *Hottonia palustris* L.
¹/₄ nat. size

Greater Bladderwort, *Utricularia vulgaris* L.

Habitat

In still water, marshes, ditches, slow reaches of river.

Botanical Features

The Greater Bladderwort is an insect-eating plant. It overwinters by means of winter buds consisting of small leaflets compacted into a sphere. The plants have no roots, and are free-floating, submerged and only the long-stalked inflorescences of loose racemes rise above water.

120

Greater Bladderwort
Utricularia vulgaris L.
$^1/_3$rd nat. size

The leaves are richly dissected and bear many bladders (utriculi), which serve to catch small aquatic animals. The stalked golden-yellow flowers resemble those of Labiatae. Flowers June–August.

Importance for fishing

Like all flaccid submerged plants the Greater Bladderwort has many useful properties. If it occurs in profusion in breeding ponds or spawning areas, it should be noted whether the traps of the plant present any danger to animal plankton or fish fry.

Shore-weed, *Littorella uniflora* (L.) Aschers

Habitat

In sandy or muddy margins of non-calcareous lakes and pools.

Shore-weed
Littorella uniflora (L.) Aschers
$^1/_2$ nat. size

Botanical Features

The plant is perennial. It reaches 2–12 cm in height. The 4–10 basal leaves are awl-shaped; the outer ones cylindrical, the inner ones roughly half-round in cross section. The male flowers are long-stalked. The corolla has 4 points; the stamens are long-stalked. The female flowers are found at the base of the stalk of the male ones. Flowers June–August.

Water Lobelia, *Lobelia dortmanna* L.

Habitat

Locally common in stony lakes and tarns in mountain areas.

122

Water Lobelia
Lobelia dortmanna L.
nat. size

Botanical Features

Plant perennial, with submerged leaf rosette. Leaves about 3–7 cm long, linear, dark green, margin entire, only frequently slightly toothed towards tip. The flower stalk rises above water surface. It bears 3–8 pale-blue flowers arranged in a loose raceme. Flowers June–August.

Importance for fishing

The plant indicates water poor in chalk.

BIBLIOGRAPHY

Allen, G.O., 1950, *British Stoneworts*. Haslemere Natural History Society, Surrey

Arber, A., 1920, *Water Plants*. Cambridge University Press

Butcher, R.W., 1933, Fishermen's Weed: Water Plants and their relation to fisheries. *Salmon and Trout Magazine*, June & September. (Reprinted and issued as a separate publication by Messrs. Sherratt & Hughes, Manchester)

Butcher, R.W., 1933, Studies on the Ecology of Rivers: 1. On the distribution of macrophytic vegetation in the rivers of Britain. *Journal of Ecology*, Vol. xxi No.1. pp.58–91

Chancellor, A.P., 1958. *The Control of Aquatic Weeds and Algae*, (Ministry of Agriculture, Fisheries and Food publication) H.M. Stationery Office

Clapham, A.R., Tutin, T.G., and *Warburg, E.F.*, 1962, *Flora of the British Isles*, 2nd Edition. Cambridge University Press

Jones, H., 1955, Notes on the identification of some British species of *Callitriche. Watsonia*, Vol.3, Pt.4. pp.186–192

Rose, F., 1965, *The Observer's Book of Grasses, Sedges & Rushes*. Warne

Sculthorpe, C.D., 1967, *The Biology of Aquatic Vascular Plants*. Edward Arnold (Publishers) Ltd

Williams, I.A., 1946, *Flowers of Marsh and Stream*. King Penguin

INDEX

Figures in bold type indicate illustrations.

Acorus calamus L. 52, **53**
Actinastrum **17**
Alisma plantago-aquatica L. 37, **38**
Amphibious Bistort 86, **87**
Anabaena **17**
Aphanizomenon 15, **17**
Arrow-head 37, **39**
Asterionella **17**
Attached organism **18**
Azolla filiculoides Lam. 80, **81**

Bacteria 15
Berula erecta (Huds.) Coville 66, 67
Bidens cernua L. 79
Bidens tripartita L. **79**
Bitter-cress, Large **63**
Bittersweet **77**
Bladderwort 120, **121**
Blue-green Algae 15, **17**
Bog Arum 50, **53**
Bogbean 69, **71**
Brooklime **78**
Bulrush 46, **48**
Glaucous 49
Bur-marigold 79
Nodding 79
Trifid **79**
Bur-reed 35, **36**
Unbranched 35, **38**
Butomus umbellatus L. **39**, 40

Calla palustris L. 50, **53**
Callitriche L. 114
Callitriche hermaphroditica L. 114, **115**
Callitriche palustris L. **115**, 116
Callitriche platycarpa, Kütz **115**, 116

Callitriche stagnalis Scop. **115**, 116
Caltha palustris L. 56, **57**
Canadian Pondweed 108, **109**
Cardamine amara L. **63**
Carex L. 49
Carex acuta L. 50, **51**
Carex pseudocyperus L. 50
Carex riparia Curtis 50
Carex rostrata Stokes 50
Ceratium **17**
Ceratophyllum demersum L. **111**
Ceratophyllum submersum L. 112
Chara spp. 95
Chlorophyceae 16, **17**
Cicuta virosa L. 63, **64**
Cladophora 16, **18**, **19**
Common Skull-cap 72, **73**
Common Spike-rush **48**, 49
Cowbane 63, **64**
Creeping Jenny **68**
Cyanophyceae 15, **17**

Diatoma **17**
Diatoms 16, **17**, **18**
Dinobryon **17**
Duckweeds **85**
Gibbous **86**
Great **86**
Ivy **86**
Least **86**

Elatine hydropiper L. 116, **117**
Eleocharis acicularis (L.) Roem & Schult 109, **110**
Eleocharis palustris (L.) Roem & Schult **48**, 49
Eleodea canadensis Michaux 108, **109**
Equisetum 31

Equisetum fluviatile L. 31, **32**
Equisetum palustre L. 31, **32**
Eudorina **17**

Fairy Moss 80, **81**
Flag 52
  Sweet 52, **53**
  Yellow 54, **55**
Flagellates 15, **17**
Floating Crystalwort 80, **81**
Flote-grass 46, **47**
Fontinalis antipyretica L. **97**
Fringed Water-lily 93, **94**
Frog-bit **84**

Gipsy-wort **75**
Glyceria fluitans (L.) R. Br. 46, **47**
Glyceria maxima (Hartm.) Holmb. 44, **45**
Great Spearwort 56, **58**
Great Water Dock 56, **57**
Great Water Grass 44, **45**
Great Yellow-cress **59**
Greater Bladderwort 120, **121**
Green Algae 16, **17**

Hippuris vulgaris L. 61, **62**
Holly-leaved Naiad **106**
Hornwort 18, **111**
  Spineless 112
Horsetail 31
  Marsh 31, **32**
  Water 31, **32**
Hottonia palustris L. 118, **120**
Hydrocharis morsus-ranae L. **84**

Iris pseudacorus L. 54, **55**
Isoetes lacustris L. **98**

Juncus 52
Juncus conglomeratus L. 54, **55**
Juncus effusus L. 54
Juncus inflexus L. 54

Kingcup 56, **57**

Lemna gibba L. **85**, 86
Lemna minor L. **85**
Lemna polyrrhiza **85**, 86
Lemna trisulca L. **85**, 86
Littorella uniflora (L.) Aschers 121, **122**
Lobelia dortmanna L. 122, **123**
Loosestrife 61
  Purple 61, **62**
  Tufted 69, **70**
  Yellow 69, **70**
Lycopus europaeus L. **75**
Lysimachia nummularia L. **68**
Lysimachia vulgaris L. 69, **70**
Lythrum salicaria L. 61, **62**

Mare's-tail 61, **62**
Marsh Marigold 56, **57**
Marsh Woundwort **74**
Melosira **17**
Menanythes trifoliata L. 69, **71**
Mentha aquatica L. **76**
Microcystis 15, **17**
Myosotis scorpioides 71, **72**
Myriophyllum spicatum L. 118, **119**
Myriophyllum verticillatum L. 117

Najas marina L. **106**
Naumburgia thyrsiflora (L.) Reichenbach 69, **70**
Nitella spp. **95**
Nuphar lutea (L.) Smith 89, **90**
Nymphaea alba L. 87, **88**
Nymphoides peltata (Gmel.) O. Kuntze 93, **94**

Oenanthe aquatica (L.) Poiret 66, **67**
Oscillatoria 15

Pediastrum **17**

126

Phalaris arundinacea L.   40, **41**
Phragmites communis Trinius 42, **43**
Phytoplankton   14, **17**
Plankton   14
Polygonum amphibium L.   86
Polygonum hydropiper L.   56, **57**
Pond-sedge, Great   50
Pondweeds   99
  Broad-leaved   **82**
  Canadian   108, **109**
  Curly   **102**
  Fennel-leaved   **105**
  Grass-wrack   **103**
  Grassy   **104**
  Perfoliate   **101**
  Shining   **100**
  Various-leaved   **83**
Potamogeton   99
Potamogeton compressus L.   **103**
Potamogeton crispus L.   **102**
Potamogeton gramineus L.   **83**
Potamogeton lucens L.   **100**
Potamogeton natans L.   **82**
Potamogeton obtusifolius Mert. et Koch   **104**
Potamogeton pectinatus L.   **105**
Potamogeton perfoliatus L.   **101**

Quillwort   **98**

Ranunculus spp.   91
Ranunculus aquatilis L.   **91**, 92
Ranunculus circinatus Sibth.   **113**
Ranunculus fluitans Lamarck   112, **113**
Ranunculus lingua L.   56, **58**
Reed   42, **43**
Reed-grass   40, **41**
Reedmace   33
  Great   33, **34**
  Lesser   33, **34**
Riciella fluitans L.   80, **81**
Rorippa amphibia (L.) Bess   **59**

Rorippa nasturtium-aquaticum (L.) Hay   **60**
Rumex hydrolaphatum Hudson   56, **57**
Rushes   52
  Conglomerate   54, **55**
  Flowering   **39**, 40
  Hard   54
  Soft   54

Sagittaria sagittifolia L.   37, **39**
Salvinia natans, Allioni   80, **81**
Scenedusmus   **17**
Schoenoplectus lacustris (L.) Palla   46, **48**
Schoenoplectus tabernaemontani   49
Scolochloa festucacea Link.   44, **45**
Scutellaria galericulata L.   72, **73**
Sedges   49
  Beaked   50
  Cyperus   50
  Tufted   50, **51**
Shore-weed   121, **122**
Sium latifolium L.   64, **65**
Slender Spike-rush   109, **110**
Solanum dulcamara L.   **77**
Sparganium emersum Rehm.   35, **38**
Sparganium erectum L.   35, **36**
Spirogyra   16, **19**
Stachys palustris (L.)   **74**
Starworts   114
  Autumnal   114, **115**
  Water   114
Stoneworts   **95**
Stratiotes aloides L.   **107**

Trapa natans L.   92, **93**
Typha   33
Typha angustifolia L.   33, **34**
Typha latifolia L.   33, **34**

Utricularia vulgaris L.   120, **121**

Veronica anagallis-aquatica L.   78
Veronica beccabunga L.   78

Water bloom   15
Water Chestnut   92, 93
Water-cress   60
Water-Crowfoots   91
  Long-leaved   112
  Stiff-leaved   113
Water Dropwort, Fine-leaved
      66, 67
Water Fern   80, 81
Water Forget-me-not   71, 72
Water-lily   87
  Fringed   93, 94
  White   87, 88
  Yellow   89, 90

Water Lobelia   122, 123
Water-milfoil   18, 117
  Spiked   118, 119
  Whorled   117
Water Mint   76
Water-parsnip   64, 65
  Narrow-leaved   66, 67
Water-pepper   56, 57
Water Plantain   37, 38
Water Soldier   107
Water Speedwell   78
Water Violet   118, 120
Waterwort   116, 117
Willow Moss   97
Wolffia arrhiza (L.) Hook ex
      Wimm   85, 86
Woody Nightshade   77